I'll cook
You take the garbage out!

Roger Cortes

Cover design by Bud Jarrin

Order this book online at www.trafford.com
or email orders@trafford.com

Most Trafford titles are also available at major online book retailers.

Print information available on the last page.

ISBN: 978-1-4120-1102-0 (sc)
ISBN: 978-1-4907-7232-5 (e)

Trafford rev. 04/05/2016

www.trafford.com
North America & international
toll-free: 1 888 232 4444 (USA & Canada)
fax: 812 355 4082

TABLE OF CONTENTS

For the Game

Sandwiches

Dinner Time

Breakfast

For the Kids

Dedicated to my daughters Nicole and Danielle who are the sweetest treats I've ever been given, and whom I love more than life itself.

I.

*** *"Shameful...tasteless... What does humping a monkey have to do with cooking?"* Juile Childless

*** *" That bastard says bam one more time I'll kick his stones up a notch!"* Ameril LaCrosse

*** *" I could have written this. Not one recipe for bananas."* Bonzo the Chimp

*** *" The jokes after the recipes are like whipped cream on dog shit."* T. Porter

*** *" Mmrpff mrfph. Mrrumm mrff ruff, burp, the sexist pig!"* Matha Burkes

Authors note: No animals were harmed in the making of this book, other than the ones we ate.

II.

ACKNOWLEDGEMENTS

There's a lot of people who need to be acknowledged and thanked for their help in getting this labor of love completed. I thank them in no particular order as each of their contributions were equally important and necessary to complete this book. So I'll just ramble them out as they come to mind. First of all, my daughter Niki who let me commandeer her computer after I crashed and burned mine. And my daughter Dani who would pull me away from this thing to go hit a few golf balls. They are my sanity. I love you girls.

Next would be Missy, my main squeeze. The woman with the patience of a saint. I don't know how she put up with me through the building of this book. Everyday she would read, correct, type and organize for me. She is also the one that road tested all the recipes. So we put on about ten pounds. It was a lot of fun. Now that it's done I will publicly admit that she is; 1). A way better typist than me, 2). Knows ten times more about computers than I will know in five life times, and 3). Was right about most of the arguments we had about this book. Thank you Miss for your endless encouragement.

III.

My best buddy, Philly B. who never missed a day without asking, "How's the book coming?" His enduring loyalty and friendship and his unmatchable sense of humor were an impetus for me. Hey Phil, up yours, I finally finished one.

Another best buddy that needs to be thanked; Rod, a.k.a. Thurston. You and I and anyone who knows you are aware of your contributions not only to this book but to my life in general. Besides all that mushy shit, you are hands down the best drinking buddy a guy could ever ask for. Thanks for your belief in me as a friend and for making my life easier.

I can't forget Joe. Thanks for the bullet-proof read buddy. I'm a lucky guy to have you as a friend. Joe is my "negative." All the things I am, he is not. All the things he is, I am not. Yet we are the same person. Go figure. So thanks to you my golf, dart, thinking and drinking partner.

My buddy Rocky. Hey pal, we don't hang as much as we should, but when we do, it's all good. I'd walk through the gates of hell with you and thumb my nose at the devil.

I would be remiss if I did not thank McCabe, the mother of my daughters. Thank you Marie for my girls, my greatest gift. Thank you for trying to understand me and for always remaining my friend.

IV.

Last, but certainly not least, I thank all my loyal customers at McCabe's, my bar and grill. Your support, friendship and good times is what makes it soooo worthwhile to be in the business. It's a lucky guy that looks forward to going to work. I'm that lucky guy.

So to all of you I wish you the only thing that matters in life, health and happiness!

SALUTE AND BON APPETIT!!!

INTRODUCTION

Ok, so why would I need a cookbook, and why would I buy one. If you're reading this and you're single you might be thinking, "that's what they make deli's and take out places for. Hell I can nuke a can of ravioli or chili and have my meal in under two minutes. Hey, if I want to get adventurous I can go for the mac and cheese or hamburger helper. Or, if I want to show off my culinary expertise, I could boil up some number nine (spaghetti) and dump a pile of one of the hundreds of jarred sauces on it. Buy a prebagged salad, a loaf of Italian bread and Bam! (Am I allowed to say that?) I'm Guiseppi Pastoroni, world famous chef. True, true a very valid argument. I too lived like that for quite some years. And to tell the truth, I still dig an occasional out of the box dinner. But take my word, it'll get old sooner or later. And believe me, it doesn't impress the babes all that much. Ok, if you are a babe, excuse me, a lady, and you're reading this, I might just as well get the apology done with now. I am more than pleased that you have even picked up this book. I would be even more thrilled if you bought it. But truth be known, this is a kinda male oriented cookbook. I'm sure I'm gonna piss off a few babes. Heck, I'm a guy, and I occasionally flip through the pages of Cosmo. Lot's of stuff in that magazine pisses me off. Though usually not the pictures. So - please accept my humblest apology right now, cause this is the last one. Let my testosterone run free throughout these pages. Hey, after all, if you look at the big picture this book is for you, the queen bee, and we, your humble workers, are just trying to impress and please you. Now that that's out of my system let's get on with it. How about you married guys, or the boys out there in limbo that have been engaged for say somewhere between three and forty seven years. And let's include in this group, da-da-da-dah, dads. Picture this; it's any ole day of the week and you get home an hour (yeah, an hour is all it takes), before "she who must be obeyed does". She walks in and smells this potpourri of flavors wafting through the house. Accustomed as she is to smelling stale beer, cigarettes and perhaps an overdue litter box, she has a perplexed look on her face as she follows her nose to the kitchen where, in all it's majesty, laid out perfectly on the table is a veritable banquet prepared for her. I'd bet she would just sh.., I mean, be really surprised. After she enjoyed this feast and stopped looking in the closets for ex-girlfriends she would be quite impressed and very thankful. You know they say the way to a man's heart is through his stomach; I believe the way to a woman's heart, and points further south, is through her stomach as well. Kids, for those of you who have kids. These days I know just as many men who prepare meals for their kids as women. I have learned from personal experience that kids will eat more than just hot dogs, french fries and pizza. Once you break them out of that routine you'll find they are more apt to say "what's for dinner?", rather than "can I have pizza?". Last, but not least, you. Hey if I came home every night to a home cooked dinner you could bet your sweet ass it would be many moons between the times that I settled for a can of ravioli for dinner. Ah, but you say I have to do the work. Take my word, its not that much work. The benefits far outweigh the work.

*****A guy and his buddy are driving through downtown Philly one night going slightly over the speed limit. A cop pulls him over and approaches the car. The driver rolls the window down. The cop says "License and registration." As the man leans over to get his wallet out the cop hits him in the head with the flashlight. "What was that for?" the guy asks. "You're in Philly pal," the cop says. "When we pull you over you don't make us wait; you have your papers ready". The cop looks at the papers and says, "Alright I'm gonna let you go, slow down." Then he walks around to the other side of the car and tells the passenger to roll down his window. The passenger complies and the cop hits him in the head with the flashlight. "What was that for?" the guy asks. "I'm just granting your wish," the cop says. I know as soon as you get about a mile down the road you're gonna say, 'boy I wish that mother fucker had tried that on me.' "

So before we begin let me tell you a few things about this book. First of all, all the recipes in this book are my own. Just as with any story, joke or musical note its all been done before. My recipe for chili may be the same as a thousand others, after all there's only so many things you can put in chili and still have it taste like chili. The same goes for my beef, chicken or fish dishes. Even soups. It has all been done before. But they are my recipes. When I started cooking some thirty years ago I learned my basics working with the pros. Whether it was at a restaurant, deli, bakery, or fast food joint you have to start somewhere. Over the years I've added my own touches, flavors and system for cooking. All changes were made according to how I liked things to taste, as well as to how people responded. You will make your changes too. In the beginning the response might have been, " That's pretty good." That wasn't good enough for me. Then it was, "Wow, that's good". That was a little better. Eventually, when I finally opened my own place it was, "Could you tell me how to make that?" So that's what I'm doing here. I'm going to tell you how to make that. I am not a world-renowned chef; nor do I ever intend to be one. (They're kinda weird anyway.) If you want to be a chef go to school. The main difference between a cook and a chef is that chefs swear in French. What I am is a cook. Cooking is a way of life for me. At home it is for my family's benefit. Outside of home it is a wonderful social event. Whether it is pleasing people in my restaurant or showing off at one of the numerous parties I attend, (if you're a decent cook you get invited to lots of parties), it's always enjoyable.

Secondly, throughout this book, I have included many of my favorite quotes, quips and jokes just to lighten things up a bit. I'll take credit for some of the quotes and quips, but as for the jokes, I stole them all. If I know who wrote them I will give credit where it is due. If I do not know, which is the case with most of them, hey, thanks for the material whoever you are.

Last but not least; this book is mostly about cooking, eating and enjoying it. For your convenience I have broken it up into different categories based on needs or desires. Also, for the convenience of those of us who are over forty and need reading glasses I've gone with a large print. If you just need glasses for reading and try to cook with them on you will find it quite difficult. Never mind the steam on the lenses, the distortion your plate will take on at countertop length is enough to make you think your parents were right about those things you used to smoke, eat or otherwise ingest. Want to see what I mean? Put your glasses on and have a close look at a sausage. Whoa! See what I mean. And please don't tell me you're wearing one of those little around the neck attach to the frame string thingy's. I'll lose my appetite. Now go have a beer.

*****A man walks into a patent office, walks up to the desk, and places a loaf of bread before the man behind the desk. "Can I help you", the man behind the desk asks. "Yes," the other says. "I'd like to patent this loaf of bread." "I'm sorry sir," the man behind the desk says. "You can't get a patent for a recipe for a loaf of bread". "Oh but this is special bread the man says. It tastes like pussy. Here, have a bite". He hands the bread to the patent man. Reluctantly the patent man takes a bite. "Pfttt," the patent man spits the bread out. "This taste like shit," he hollers. "Oh, my bad," the other man says. "Turn it over."

GETTING STARTED

I can't cook! I hear it all the time. It's amazing, really. You can't expect me to believe that let's say an engineer, a guy who designs and builds bridges, can't put a meatloaf together. Or how about a fireman who climbs a hundred foot ladder, jumps into a burning building, hoists a four hundred pound, ahem, lady, over his shoulder and carries her out. Can't be afraid of the stove. Guys in all walks of life, in every imaginable trade say they can't cook. There's only one word for that...Bullshit! I can understand some guys don't want to cook but you're obviously not one of them or you wouldn't be this far into this book. Unless of course you're just here for the dirty jokes. If that's the case, by all means read on. There are plenty of them here. For the rest of you guys I'm gonna ease you into this real slow

Here's a list of what you need to get started as far as utensils go. I am assuming of course that you do have running water and a stove/oven. You do, don't you? Well in the event that you don't, before going any further in this book I would like to recommend you watch one of my favorites, "Quest for Fire". You do have a VCR don't you?

So here we go...

1. A set of pots and pans. T-Fal makes several different varieties. I use them at home. The reason I recommend them is that they are strong, long lasting and very affordable. They have withheld the test of time and training my daughters to cook. I have seen that it is possible to weld ground beef to any cooking surface. In all seriousness I have not been compensated for mentioning the brand T-Fal. What I have stated about them is true. (Though I would not be abject to any future comps if you folks from T-Fal are reading this.) So... did I mention T-Fal as my brand of choice? A decent set of T-Fals (seven to nine piece) runs about seventy bucks. That set will usually include a few pans, pots and utensils. Also, spring for another thirty bucks and pick yourself up a decent eight to twelve quart cooking pot. You will need it sooner or later.

2. A GOOD set of knives. Don't go cheap. Good knives will hold their edge much longer. Also with the knives make sure you get a steel. Those are the long file looking things you see the TV cooking stars sharpening their knives on. Or you could just poke your head in the window of any butcher department and see them in action. Cooking with dull knives is time consuming frustrating and dangerous. I don't recommend any particular brand. I like Polli, Grohmann or Forschner. Yeah I know, I might as well have Said Moe, Larry and

Curleys. Fact is, the best way to figure out what brand to get is to ask any butcher. You really only need two cooking knives. One eight inch for general purpose, and maybe a paring knife. Good knives aren't cheap. The two I mention should run about seventy-five bucks, but worth every penny and will last forever.

3. Cutting boards. Very simple, very cheap. I recommend two - one small, about 6"x10" and one large - about 12"x18". Definitely go for the Teflon boards. They are easy to clean and they last forever. Wood boards may look fancy, but they basically suck. They don't clean very easily and they scar easily. They warp and they hold germs. 'Nuf said. Both boards will cost you under twenty dollars. I guess in this category I should also recommend a measuring cup and spoons. I rarely use them except in baking but in the beginning you might find them helpful.

4. Perishables: These things you should always have on hand and if you do you'll be able to prepare most of the entrees in this book. Flour, breadcrumbs, oil and spices. The main spices are - salt, pepper, cumin, celery salt, paprika, cayenne, garlic (crushed in oil and granulated), oregano, chili powder, basil, parsley flakes, beef and chicken base. Total should run about fifty bucks and they will last you through many meals.

So there you have it. Your starter kit all for roughly the same price as one good night at Tempting Tanya's House of Ta-ta's.

*****A guy walks into a bar. "Get me a shot of whiskey and a beer, get everyone a drink on me, and don't forget yourself", he says to the bartender. When the bartender is finished serving everyone he pours himself a drink, walks over to the generous guy, and thanks him. "That'll be twenty-seven bucks buddy", he says. "Damn I forgot my wallet," the guy says. "Get outta here you asshole", the bartender says. The guy leaves. Two weeks later the same guy comes in. "Get me a shot of whiskey and a beer, get everyone a drink on me, and don't forget yourself", he says to the bartender. "You have your wallet this time?" the bartender asks. "Sure do," the guy says, and places his wallet on the bar. The bartender pours everyone a drink and makes himself one. He walks over to the guy and says, "that'll be forty-five dollars."
"I don't have any money," the guy says. With that the bartender gets so mad he jumps over the bar, punches the guy in the face and drags him by his jacket out the door. Two weeks later the guy comes back in. He puts a hundred dollar bill on the bar and says, "Get me a shot of whiskey and a beer and get everybody in the bar a drink on me." "Aren't you gonna buy me a drink?" the bartender asks. "Nah," the guy says. "You get nasty when you drink."

SOUPS, SALADS, SIDES, AND SUCH

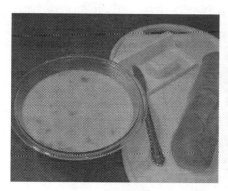 

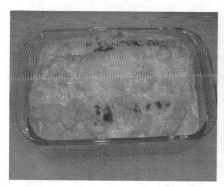 

RICE

Now listen up! I know you're probably saying what kind of moron does this guy think I am. Not true. Rice may be the simplest thing to make but I have seen more pots of mush than the Little Rascals have. Forget about what the box or bag says, (I'm referring to white rice, not all the mixed varieties.) and listen to me. Don't buy cheap rice. Hey, you don't buy cheap beer. As in pretty much everything, if you start with a decent product, odds are you'll end up with a decent product if you know what you're doing. Besides, rice is one of the best bargains out there. Even the good stuff is affordable. OK, here we go.
You will need:
2 cups of rice
1 tbsp. oil
1 tsp. salt
3 3/4 cups water
Duct tape

Step 1. Put a piece of duct tape over any directions on the bag or box.
Step 2. In a pot, pour one tablespoon of oil and one teaspoon of salt. Add two cups of rice, turn on the heat to medium high and stir. When the rice is coated with oil and salt add 3 3/4 cups of water. (I know, I know, the

bag/box says 2 cups of water for each cup of rice. That's where all the mush comes from. So put the duct tape back and listen to me).

Step 3. Turn the heat on high and bring to a boil. Once the kettle is boiling give it one last stir, cover the pot and drop your heat as low as it will go. Then go have a beer for about 12 to 15 minutes. DO NOT take the cover off and stir. Totally unnecessary. After your cook time is done you'll know the rice is done when you remove the lid and there is no more water. Just a nice flat layer of rice with all these crater looking holes on the top.

Rice is a great complement to any entree. It goes well with beef, chicken, pork and fish. It's great to add to soup and makes a nice bed for Chili. You can do lots of things to vary your flavors of rice. You can throw just about anything in it you like. I like to throw a handful of diced onions and some crushed garlic in mine. Perhaps a touch of paprika for red rice, or saffron for yellow. You can add these things while your bringing the pot to a boil. It won't ruin the texture of your rice. Or if you prefer you can sauté stuff and add it after. Go on now, make a pot of rice and throw some weird stuff in it.

*****A grasshopper walks into a bar, grabs a seat and calls the bartender over for a drink. The bartender sees the grasshopper and says, "Hey, I make a drink named after you". "Oh yeah," says the grasshopper. "What do you put in an Irving?"

GARLIC PARMESAN NOODLES

This is a side dish I invented when about 20 more people than I expected showed up for a dinner. I had little time and less options. Fortunately I had a few pounds of egg noodles lying around. I guess it worked. I got a lot of compliments and even a request for the recipe. Unfortunately I had no fucking clue what I did. Since then I've figured it out. It didn't take an Einstein. Nice and simple.

You will need:

1 lb. bag of egg noodles
1 stick of butter
1/2 cup Parmesan cheese
2 tbsp. crushed garlic
1tbsp. Olive oil

In a pot bring six quarts of water to a boil. Dump the noodles in and cook them. Do not over-cook them. Let them stay firm. When they are cooked drain the water and put the noodles in a bowl. Add 1 tbsp. Olive oil and the stick of butter. Stir it around until the butter is melted. Now just stir your garlic and cheese in and it's done. Like I said, it don't take an Einstein.

*****A ten year old kid was sitting on a bench next to an old man gobbling down a large bag of candy. "You know," the old man said, "eating all that candy is not good for you. It's very unhealthy." "My grandfather lived to be 94" the boy replied. "Oh," the old man replied. "He ate a lot of candy too?" "No," the boy replied. "He minded his own fucking business."

McCABE'S BAR AND GRILL

CHEESE POTATOES

This is a good side dish that goes with just about everything. Make lots cause I'm sure the kids will ask for more.

You will need:
3 lbs. of potatoes
12 oz. shredded cheddar cheese
1 stick of butter
1 pint of sour creme
3 tbsps. of flour
1 tbsp. crushed garlic
1/2 tsp. salt
1/4 tsp. pepper

Peel the potatoes, chop them into chunks (1 inch chunks), and boil them until they are soft. In the meantime melt the butter and cheese in a saucepan. In a bowl mix the sour creme, flour and spices. Add the melted butter and cheese to the bowl and mix thoroughly. Now stir in the potatoes and place everything in a casserole dish, cover and bake in the oven for 20 - 30 minutes at 350 degrees.

*****A guy steps into an elevator. As he's reaching to press the floor button, he accidentally hit the lady standing next to him in her breast with his elbow. "I'm really sorry," he says to the lady, " but if your heart is as soft as your breasts, I know you'll forgive me." "Mister," replies the lady, "if your dick is as hard as your elbow, I'm in room 363."

STUFFING

Hey, if you want to be the big shot at Thanksgiving dinner don't just carve the bird, cook it and while you're at it make the stuffing too. Though turkeys and chicken are easy to do, in fact they tell you how on most of the wrappings they come in, stuffing is a different matter all together. It really can make the dinner. Here's a recipe I learned from my mom that goes over really well.

You will need:

3 loaves of bread

1 large onion

4 stalks of celery

8oz. Sage sausage (breakfast sausage tube style package)

4 cups of chicken broth

1 tbsp. of garlic

1/2 tsp. of salt

1/4 tsp. of pepper

Giblets from the bird (optional)

Dice the onion and celery. Tear the bread into two-inch pieces. Put this stuff in a bowl. Add the four cups of chicken broth. Ground the sausage to the consistency of taco meat and lightly brown it in a pan. If you're going to use the giblets dice them up and brown them with the sausage. Don't overcook this stuff, in fact keep it a little on the rare side. It's going in the oven anyway and you don't want to dry it out. When it is browned dump it, grease and all, into the bowl. Add the rest of the spices and mix thoroughly. Now if you have a bird stuff as much as you can right up the ole wazul. Since a bird's butt can only hold X amount of stuffing put the rest in a baking tray and cover with foil. The stuffing in the bird will cook right along with the bird. If you're not stuffing a bird or if you have that extra tray, cook it in the oven at 375 degrees for an hour.

*****A guy comes walking out of the store and he sees this cop writing a ticket for parking in the fire lane. "Hey, give a guy a break would you," he says to the cop. But the cop just continues to write the ticket. " You Nazi bastard," the guy says just loud enough for the cop to hear. The cop does hear him so he starts writing a ticket for a bald tire. "What a prick" the guy says. The cop hears him again and starts to write another ticket for a tiny crack in the windshield. "I could do this all day," the cop says. "Knock yourself out," the guy says. "I'm parked around the corner."

MACARONI SALAD

Everybody should know how to make a few good salads. You know, it's decided everyone's going to Rich's house for the game and instead of bringing chips you just go like "hey, I got the salads." It's cool. So anyway this is another of those quick and easy recipes. You starting to notice a pattern yet?

You will need: (for like 8 guys or 3 guys named Beef)

1lb. box or bag of elbow macaroni
1 small onion
1 small bell pepper
1/2 carrot
2 stalks of celery
1 cup of mayo
Salt and pepper

In a pot put about 4 quarts of water over a high flame. Throw a little splash of oil in the water. When the water is boiling put the mac elbows in. While you're waiting for the macaroni to cook dice up your onions, peppers, carrots and celery. When the elbows are cooked, drain the water and rinse the bows with cold water. Shake off all the water or you'll have macaroni soup. Those little suckers can hide the water inside and I've seen many a bowl of slop. So anyway, put your elbows in a bowl. Now don't you feel fucking ridiculous? Not those elbows, the MACARONI elbows. You know, the one's you just cooked. Add all your diced veggies and mayo. Give it a good mixing. Add a little salt and pepper and give it another good mixing. With salads like this it's so easy to kill them with salt and pepper so I recommend you go slowly with them and stop when you like the way it tastes.

*****A guy walks into the employment office. When he gets to the window the man behind the glass asks "How may I help you?" "Well," the guy on line replies, "I need a job. I want my self-respect. I've been working the system for as long as I can remember. My whole family is on welfare and it goes all the way back to my grandparents. I've had enough. I want to earn my own keep!" "Well you're in luck," the employment man says. "I've got something here. Let's see, it's driving this little old lady around, you know, to the grocery store, or church, etc. AND it pays $100,000 a year with benefits and paid vacation and holidays." "You're bullshitting me!" The man on line says with obvious excitement. "Well you started it," the employment man replied.

THE POORBOYS: from left to right: (seated) Brooklyn, Sly, Julio, Philly B., Mr. Bun, Stryker, and Attie, the Incredible Pond Scum Queen.

POTATO SALAD

Potato salad is a party favorite. Everybody likes to brag about his or her potato salad. If not their own, then their wife's or their Aunt Mabel's, blah, blah, blah. If you start with potatoes and throw some stuff in it you got potato salad. So, here's my recipe, which by the way, is the best in the universe.

You will need:

3lbs. white or red potatoes (about 8 or nine medium sized)

1 onion about the size of a tennis ball

4 stalks of celery

1 cup of mayo

6 strips of bacon (don't use fake bacon, it sucks)

4 eggs

1 tbsp. mustard (regular ole mustard)

1 tsp. salt

1/4 tsp. pepper

Get a good-sized pot and bring some water to a boil. Since that's gonna take a while start peeling those potatoes. After you've peeled them cut them into chunks about the size of the ear on a six-week-old chinchilla. Just fuckin' with ya. Cut them into one to two inch chunks. When the water is boiling toss the spuds in. After about 10 minutes you can put your eggs in to hard boil. Hey it saves cleaning another pot, and the taters don't mind. Now dice the onion and celery up fairly fine. Cook up your bacon so it's nice and crispy, but don't burn it. Dice that up as well. I believe at this time it's time for a beer, cause that dicing and bacon should only take about five to ten minutes and the spuds will take 15 - 20. Ten minutes to kill. What else can you do in ten minutes? Never mind, I don't want to know. Check on your taters. Don't let them get too soft. When you can put them between your thumb and index and squeeze and they kinda split, they are ready. If they mush, throw all the other ingredients away, drain the water, add milk and butter and congratulations, you have mashed potatoes. Not a big hit at parties. Assuming that you have cooked the potatoes just right, drain the water and cool them with cold water. Shake off all the excess water and dump them in a big bowl along with everything else on the ingredient list. Oh yeah, don't forget to dice those eggs too.

*****5 best remarks ever made by a caddy:

1. Golfer: Do you think I can get there with a five iron?
   Caddy: Eventually

2. Golfer: I think I'm gonna go drown myself in that lake.
   Caddy: You think you can keep your head down that long?

3. Golfer: Please stop checking your watch all the time. It's a distraction.
   Caddy: It's not a watch, it's a compass.

4. Golfer: This is the worst course I've ever played on.
   Caddy : This isn't the course, we left that an hour ago.

5. Golfer: You've got to be the worst caddy in the world.
   Caddy: I don't think so sir, that would be too much of a coincidence.

TUNA OR EGG SALAD

Here's a little two-for recipe that should be under the category of "for those who have no clue." It's fast and easy and makes a great sandwich to pack for work or school.

You will need:
Either two 7 oz. cans of tuna or six boiled eggs
1 small onion
1 stalk of celery
4 tbsps. mayonnaise
salt and pepper

Finely dice the onion and celery and put them in a bowl. For tuna salad drain the water or oil off the tuna and add it to the bowl. For egg salad, hard boil the eggs and dice them up and add them to the bowl. If you don't know how to hard boil eggs maybe now's a good time to start collecting those Pizza Hut coupons. At any rate, for whichever you're doing, all the ingredients go in the bowl and get mixed together. It's that simple. If you want to turn the tuna salad into dinner just spread some on a hoagie roll, cover with a few slices of American cheese and melt the cheese in the oven or toaster oven. The good ole tuna melt standby. Dinner in less than 10 minutes.

*****Two Rabbis are walking down a sidewalk when they come across a sign in front of a Catholic Church. The sign reads, "Come inside and we will convert you in ten minutes or pay you ten dollars." The first Rabbi turns to the second and says, "Can you believe those Catholics? They think they can convert the whole world." "Say," says the second, "I have an idea. I'll go inside, listen to his pitch and in ten minutes I'll just tell him I'm not interested, get the ten bucks and leave." He goes inside and after ten minutes comes walking out. "Well" says the first Rabbi, "did you get the ten bucks?" The second replies, "is that all you people think about?"

RAY and MARY Back for a visit

WISCONSIN CHEDDAR CHEESE AND BEER SOUP

This would just be another sissy-assed cookbook if I didn't put at least one recipe with the word beer in the title. I like this soup, a lot. Not just because it has beer in it, but it's got great flavor and a nice little kick. And since it only requires one bottle of beer, that leaves three for you and two for your girlfriend. (You're the one doing the work.)

You will need:

1 bottle of beer (your choice)
8 oz. shredded cheddar cheese
3 medium sized potatoes
1 small onion
1 stalk of celery
1 carrot
1/2 pint heavy cream
1 tbsp. mustard
1 tsp. hot sauce
1 1/2 quarts water
2 tbsp. chicken base
1/4 stick butter
dash of salt

Dice the potatoes, onion, celery, and carrot and brown them lightly in a pan with the butter. Whisk the chicken base into the water and put it on to boil. Add the browned veggies to the water. In the same pan over a very low flame, melt the cheddar cheese and whisk the heavy cream in. When the cheese is melted add it and the remaining spices to the pot. Pour in the beer and let the soup cook for about fifteen minutes. Stir occasionally to ensure the cheese getting well mixed in.

*****God was bored so he asks St. Peter for a recommendation for a good spot to go on vacation. "How about Jupiter?" St. Peter says. "No," says God. "The gravity is tough on my old bones." "Well, how about Mercury?" St. Peter tries. "I can't take the heat," God replies. "Then what about Earth?" St. Peter asks. "Earth?" God says, "Forget Earth. The last time I was there 2000 years ago, I had a fling with this cute little Jewish girl, and they're still talking about it."

SPLIT PEA SOUP

Split pea soup is, to me, one of those mysteries of life. It is after all, just some dried peas brought back to life with a little water and boiled up with a few veggies and condiments. So why do I like it so much? You couldn't get me to eat a plate of peas if you threatened to hog tie me to a chair and listen to Boy George for a week. Still, I love the soup. Just what the hell happens to those suckers when you add a few extras to the pot? Sweet mysteries of life.

You will need:

1lb bag of split peas

1 good sized onion

2 stalks of celery

1/2 carrot

1/2 lb ham (get the slab, not sliced)

1 tbsp. (heaping) chicken base (or 3 bouillons)

1/2 tsp salt

1/4 tsp pepper

The pain in the ass about this soup is strictly the split peas. They are like the end of the season Mets. You never know what's gonna happen. Some peas will soften a whole lot quicker than others. I don't know the science behind figuring that out. I do know I have the best success with a good brand such as Goya. I'll tell you to start off by putting 8 - 10 cups of water in the pot along with the peas. Dice up your onions, carrot, celery and ham and toss them in. Add the rest of the ingredients and bring the pot to a good boil. Now reduce the heat to a simmer, cover the pot and let the soup continue to cook for an hour. In one hour your soup should be ready. The key word here being should. I'm not usually that lucky. I usually have to add a bit more water and continue cooking. Sometimes two or three times, depending on the mood of the peas. I've had conversations with lots of people who make great pea soup and we all encounter the same problem. But it's really not a problem; it's more of just a pain in the ass. I guarantee you one thing though; this recipe makes some kick ass pea soup.

*****A blonde was walking around a lake somewhat lost when she sees another blonde across the water. "Hey," she yells, "How do I get to the other side?" To which the other blonde responds, " You're already there."

PHILLY B., MISS and ME

33

CREAM OF BROCCOLI SOUP

Sometimes you just don't feel like a full meal and that's when having a few soup recipes comes in handy. I don't know too many guys, or gals for that matter, that take the time to make homemade soups. So what the hell, get the one up on her. Make soup.
You will need:
1 head of broccoli
1 pint of half and half
1 stick of butter
1 tbsp. chicken base
1 itsy-bitsy onion (1/4 cup)
3/4 cup flour
1/4 tsp. pepper
6 cups water

Take about 3/4 of the butter and melt it in a pan. Mix the flour with one cup of water and pour it into the butter. Put this on a low flame. You don't want it to brown, just heat up. If necessary you can turn it off while you're waiting for the rest of the recipe to catch up. Once you get the hang of this thing you'll get your timing down. I've seen my girlfriends head spin like something out of the Exorcist making the same recipes I would make with six shots of Tequila in me. (And that's keeping one hand free to hold onto the counter for dear life.) It's not a talent thing, just repetition. In a pot put the remaining butter with the finely diced onions and brown. Cut the broccoli into little heads and add to the onions. Stir until the broc gets tender. Mix the chicken base with 5 cups of water and add to the pot. Stir in the half and half. When it's good and hot slowly stir in the roux. THE WHAT? you say. The roux is that butter, water and flour mix. When it's hot enough for you it's done.

*****True Story: Frank Sinatra was coming out of a hotel casino a few years back. The bellhop set his bags down. "Hey kid," Sinatra asked. "What's the biggest tip you've ever received?" "One hundred dollars," the bellhop replied. Not to be out done Frank hands the guy two hundred dollars. "Thank you very much, Mr. Sinatra," the hop says. As Frank is walking away he stops, turns and calls to the bellhop. "Hey kid," he says. "Who gave you the hundred?" "Why that would be you Mr. Sinatra," the hop replied.

CREAM OF POTATO SOUP

Here we go again with soup. Soups require patience. I really didn't want to cover soup in this book but I was persuaded with sexual favors. Just kidding babe. I like soups. It's just that I find nothing humorous about them. It's not like pounding your chicken or beating the meat. OK, I'll grow up. Pee soup, hah, he said pee.

You will need:

3 lbs. potatoes
2 medium onions
3 cups of milk
1 pint of half and half
1/2 stick of butter
1/2 lb of bacon
1/4-cup parsley flakes
1tbsp. chicken base
1 1/2 quarts of water
1 tsp. crushed garlic
1/4 tsp. pepper

Peel and dice your potatoes. The smaller you dice them the faster they cook. I say one inch chunks. In a pot put the potatoes, water and chicken base. Boil the potatoes until they are tender which is about 20 minutes. In the mean time dice the onions and soften them in the butter. Don't brown them. If you are capable of multi-tasking, cook up the bacon, nice and crispy. When the potatoes are soft add the milk, onions, bacon, (crumbled) garlic, parsley flakes and pepper. (Phew) Simmer for about ten minutes and then stir in the half and half. Five more minutes of simmer. That ought to do it.

*****A guy walks into a pet store looking to purchase an exotic breed of dog. "I'm sorry," the owner says, "but we've had a run on dogs and I don't have a one. You want exotic? How about this monkey here?" "No," says the potential buyer, "I was just looking for a dog." "Come over here", the store owner says pulling the man to the side. "This here monkey is special. He can give you the best blowjob you ever had and I'm just asking four hundred for him." "Get the fuck outta here," the man says disgustedly. "What are you sick or something?" "Look," says the owner, "just take him home for one night and if you don't like him you can bring him back in the morning." The man crumbles under the sales pitch and leaves the store with the monkey. Later that night his wife comes home and from the kitchen she hears all sorts of racket. Dishes breaking, pans clanging, glass shattering, etc... She walks into the kitchen and sees the man and the monkey and the kitchen in a total mess. "WHAT THE FUCK IS GOING ON HERE?!!!" she screams. "Look," says the guy, jerking his thumb towards the monkey. "This thing learns how to cook, you're outta here."

My Fair Ladies; NIKI, MISSY, and DANI

CREAMY CHICKEN SOUP

This is a great winter night soup. At the risk of sounding like one of those canned soup commercials it's a soup that eats like a meal. What pisses me off is that a can of their soup runs 2 - 3 bucks and feeds maybe two. This recipe runs about 3 bucks and feeds six, with a possibility of seconds.

You will need:

1& 1/2 lbs. boned and skinned chicken
2 quarts of water
1 quart of milk
1/2 stick of butter
1 cup warm water
1/2 cup of flour
2 & 1/2 tbsps. chicken base
1 small onion
2 carrots
2 stalks of celery
salt and pepper

Put the 2 quarts of water in a pot with the base and bring to a boil. Dice the vegetables and chicken and dump them in the water. Keep this going at a rapid boil. In a saucepan melt the butter and add the milk. Keep this on a low flame for a minute or two. When the chicken is cooked and the veggies are soft (about 15 - 20 minutes) turn down the flame to a simmer and add the milk and butter. Now whisk the flour into the cup of warm water. Slowly pour the flour/water mix into the soup. Let it thicken for a few minutes. Salt and pepper to taste.

*****At the completion of a funeral service for a woman in a synagogue the pallbearers are carrying the casket out. One of them accidentally bumps a wall and they hear a moan from inside the casket. Upon opening the casket they find that the woman is still alive. She lives for another ten years then dies. At the same synagogue at the completion of the services the pallbearers are again carrying her out. As they're passing the husband he says, "Watch out for that wall."

PASTA SALAD

A good pasta salad looks like "who flung dung," which incidentally should be the name of this recipe. There are no set rules for making pasta salad, (or any dish for that matter) other than I suppose it should include pasta of some sort. I don't believe I've ever made it the same way twice so this recipe will consist of what I did the last time. I do remember it was good.

You will need:

16 oz. of uncooked ziti (or those little spiral thingys. I don't know what they are professionally called but they look like an auger bit.)

1/4 lb. ham (buy it un-sliced)

1/4 lb. cheddar cheese

1/4 lb. Munster cheese

1/4 lb. pepperoni

2 medium sized tomatoes

1 medium sized onion

2 stalks of celery

1/4 cup of grated parmesan cheese

1/4 cup each of red wine vinegar and olive oil

1 tbsp. crushed garlic

1/2 tsp. each of basil, parsley, oregano and salt

1/4 tsp. pepper

Bring four quarts of water to a boil and add the ziti. While the ziti is cooking dice the ham, cheeses, pepperoni, tomatoes, onions and celery into 1/2-inch chunks. In a large cup add all the spices to the oil and vinegar. Mix thoroughly. When the ziti is done drain the water and rinse with cool water. Again drain all the excess water. Now put the ziti in a bowl and add the chopped stuff. Stir it around and then add the oil/vinegar mixture. Sprinkle the Parmesan cheese over the top and stir until everything is evenly coated. I know it sounds like a lot of work but the whole deal takes about 15 - 20 minutes and you'll be the belle of the ball when you show up at the neighborhood barbeque with it.

*****A woman is in a Mercedes dealership walking round her dream car. She leans in through the open window and bends over to feel the leather seats. As she's bending a fart slips out. Feeling quite embarrassed she looks around to see if anyone heard it. The salesman sees her looking around and walks over to her. Trying to remain cool she asks the salesman, "How much is this lovely automobile?" "Lady," replied the salesman, "If you farted just touching it you're gonna shit when I tell you the price."

Partying at the Warehouse
Left to right; LISA, RICH, MARI, MIKE

BEEF VEGETABLE SOUP

This is another monkey recipe you can't screw up. But easy doesn't mean bad. It's a good soup and perfect for those cold winter nights. A good time to make this soup is when you have some leftover beef in the fridge. You will need:

2 quarts of water
1 lb. of beef (most any will do)
2 tbsps. beef base
1 small onion
2 stalks of celery
1 8 oz. package of whatever frozen veggie you like
salt and pepper

In a large pot bring the water and beef base to a boil. If your beef is already cooked dice it into one-inch chunks and add it to the boiling water. If the beef isn't cooked cut it into one-inch chunks, brown it lightly in a splash of oil, then add it to the water. Dice the onion and celery and add them to the pot. Let the pot go to a rolling boil for about 15 - 20 minutes. When the onions and celery are soft add the frozen veggies and turn the flame down to low. When the soup starts boiling again let it simmer for about 5 - 10 minutes. Salt and pepper to taste.

*****A guy is standing on line in a grocery store watching the girl in front of him putting her items on the conveyor belt. 1/2 dozen eggs, 1 stick of butter, a loaf of bread, a quart of milk, and a can of tuna. He turns to the girl and says, "I'll bet your single." "Why, yes I am" said the girl. "Can you tell by what I'm buying?" "No," the guy replied, "you're fucking ugly".

Just a night at the bar. Bartender CARL. Good guy, bad jersey.

GRAVY

When you're sitting down for a home cooked meal a good gravy is the finishing touch. It's real easy to make and most of the time the main dish provides most of the ingredients. The best gravy starts with the drippings off the beef, chicken or pork you just cooked. It's there, in the bottom of the pan. Unless you've murdered the main and it all cooked out. If that's the case I'll give you an emergency quick gravy recipe.

You will need:
The drippings
1 tsp. of either beef, chicken or pork base (depending on the main, duh.)
2 cups of warm water
1/2 cup of flour
pinch of pepper

Pour the drippings into a pot. Put it on a low flame. Whisk together the water, base and flour. Add this mix to the drippings and keep whisking. Add the pepper to taste. When the gravy thickens up it's done.

Now let's say that you have murdered the main as I have on occasion and there is no drippings. As long as it doesn't look like a lump of coal you can still save the dish with gravy. Here's a quick gravy.

You will need:
3 cups of water
1 cup of warm water
1/2 cup of flour
2 tbsps. of base
1 tbsp. cooking oil
pinch of pepper

In a pot bring the three cups of water to a boil.
Whisk together the base, warm water, oil and flour. Turn
down the heat and whisk the water/flour mix in. Pepper
to taste. So it's not AS good as the real thing, but it runs
a close second and could save a meal.

*****10 reasons why it's great to be a man:

1. Your last name stays the same.
2. The garage is all yours.
3. Your ass is never a factor in a job interview.
4. Car mechanics tell you the truth.
5. A week's vacation requires one suitcase.
6. You never feel compelled to stop a friend from getting laid.
7. Your underwear is $10 for a three pack.
8. You don't give a rat's ass if someone notices your new haircut.
9. Your gut usually hides your big hips.
10. You can quietly watch a ball game with a buddy for hours without ever thinking "He must be mad at me."

My friend WAYNE - He came with the place and pulled
me through the first seven years.

TOMATO SAUCE (quick sauce)

I call this sauce a quick sauce cause basically uh; it's quick to make. But we will not compromise flavor here. It's still a hearty, robust sauce and beats the hell out of anything you would pour out of a jar.
You will need:
1 medium sized onion
1 bell pepper
2-3 tbsps. crushed garlic (depending on how much you like garlic; I go with three)
1 28-oz. can of crushed tomatoes
1 28 oz. can of tomato puree
1 6oz. Can of tomato paste
1 cup of wine
1/4 cup of sugar
2 tbsps. oregano
1 tsp. basil
1/4 tsp. pepper
1 tsp. salt
Olive oil

Open your three cans and pour them into a pot. (OK, so the paste doesn't quite pour. Just get it into the pot somehow.) Turn the flame to medium and add the wine, sugar, oregano, basil, salt and pepper. Stir them in there good. Next, finely dice the onion and pepper. Coat the bottom of a pan with the olive oil and add the onion, pepper and garlic to the pan. Brown this stuff till it's kinda transparent. Don't burn it or you'll ruin everything. It should only take about fifteen minutes, on the outside, for this to be ready to add to the pot. When it's nicely browned dump the whole kit and caboodle in the pot and stir it in. *Don't drain the oil, it has a nice flavor and will give a nice texture to your sauce. When your sauce starts poppin like Vesuvius lower the flame to a simmer, cover the pot and go have a beer. Don't forget to stir every so often, and like I said before the better the pot the less you have to keep an eye on it. In about an hour your flavors should be nicely melded together and you're ready to do with it as you please. It's a great spaghetti sauce and even better if you brown up about two pounds of chopped meat and add it. If you do that, add the chop meat when you add the onions and stuff, and don't forget to drain the fat off the meat. This sauce also freezes well.

*****A guy walks into the bank and walks up to the teller's window. "May I help you?", the lady asks. "Yeah," the man replies. "I'd like to make a fucking deposit." "Excuse me", the woman says, taken back by the mans rudeness. "I said, I'd like to make a fucking deposit", the man said adamantly. "Hold on just a moment", the woman says and goes over to get the bank manager. "What's the problem?" the manager asks. "Well," says the woman, "The man at my window is being quite rude to me." " I'll handle this," the manager says as they both walk over to the rude man at the window. "Can I help you sir?" the manager says to the man. "Yeah you can," the man replies. "I just won the lottery and I want to make a fucking deposit." The manager replies, "and this bitch here is giving you a hard time?"

COCKTAIL SAUCE

If you like eating shrimp, scallops, clams and such it's a good thing to keep some cocktail sauce around the house. I know you can run out and buy a bottle sauce but that's too easy. Besides most of them are so lame you have to doctor them up anyway. On the other hand we don't want to take away precious drinking time fucking around with starting from scratch. So we'll compromise here. We'll start with catsup and run with it. I like my cocktail sauce with a kick. The kind that when it hits the back of your mouth it sets off a minor explosion in your sinuses and forces you to grab a tissue. So if you like it like that this is for you. If not you can adjust the amount of horseradish.

You will need:

1 16 oz. bottle of catsup. (buy the cheap crap, it's just a base.)

3 tbsps. of horseradish

Worcestershire sauce

1 lemon (unless you know where to buy a half)

1/4 tsp. granulated garlic

1/8 tsp. pepper

In a bowl mix together all the ingredients except the lemon. Slice the lemon in half and squeeze the juice from 1/2 the lemon in the mix. Stir again until blended.

FOR THE GAME

SALSA

This is another one of those dishes everyone should know how to make. Salsa has become so popular that it has surpassed ketchup in sales. It's fast and easy to make, goes with about everything (I put it in my omelets), and has a shelf life of about sixty years. All right, a bit of an exaggeration, but if kept covered and refrigerated it does easily last several weeks. I imagine you could even freeze it. I don't know from personal experience cause mine never lasts that long. Blah, blah, blah. I know I'm running the pie -hole a tad. I could go on forever expounding the virtues and benefits of salsa but I'm sure you'd rather just have the recipe.

You will need:

2 28oz. cans of whole peeled tomatoes

1 large onion

2 medium bell peppers

4 -6 medium jalapenos (depending on heat)

1/2 cup of hot sauce (I recommend Franks)

1 tbsp. Crushed garlic

1 tsp. salt

1/2 tsp. pepper

1/2 tsp cayenne

* You can add 1/2 tsp. of cilantro, but it's not one of those spices you keep around the house unless you do a lot of Mexican cooking. I don't use it and I don't get any complaints.

Open your cans of tomatoes and dump them, liquid and all in a pot. Stick your hand in the pot and start crushing those bad boys. I'll warn you right now those suckers are loaded and if you don't hold em' to the bottom they will explode just about everywhere, covering you and all areas in about a ten-foot radius. Break them up till they're about the size of nipples, I mean nickels. Next dice up your onion and bell peppers. Then FINELY dice the jalapenos. OK, now take those and everything else and toss it in the pot. Give it a good stir, put on a low flame, cover the pot and go call the guys and invite them over for a card game. Tell them not to forget the beer. In an hour, remove it from the flame and stick it in the fridge to cool. Bingo, that's it. Go get some chips.

*****A very large strapping woodsman--looking guy walks into a bar finds himself a place to stand right in the middle and orders a whiskey and beer. He fires them down and turns his head to the right. In a booming voice he looks down the bar and says, "You're all a bunch of motherfuckers." No one says a word. They all just look down at their drinks nervously. The woodsman orders another whiskey and beer and fires them down. He turns his head to the left and says "You're all a bunch of cocksuckers." Again no one says anything. Then a little guy stands up and walks towards the man. "You have a problem with what I said?" The woodsman asks. "No," replied the little guy, "I was just sitting on the wrong side of the bar."

Chili

Every guy that's ever thought about even walking into a kitchen should know how to make a decent Chili. There are probably more recipes out there for Chili than any other substance known to man. But they all start out the same basically. Tomatoes, peppers, onions and Chili powder. If you don't have those four ingredients in there you're not making Chili. You can call it Chili if you want, but it ain't. This Chili I'm gonna give you is easy, fast and has won me a couple of trophies at Chili cook-offs.

You will need:

1 28oz. can of diced tomatoes
1 28 oz can of tomato puree
1 28oz. can of red kidney beans (optional)
2 good sized onions
2 decent sized bell peppers
4 - 6 jalapenos (depending on how spicy you like it)
2 lbs of ground beef
1 tbsp. of crushed garlic
1/3 cup Chili powder
1 tsp. Salt and pepper.

In a pot dump your tomatoes, puree and kidney beans. (don't forget to drain the liquid off the beans first.) Julienne cut your onions and bell peppers and add them. Cut the stems off the jalapenos and dice them up real fine. Leave the seeds; they add a nice kick. Next, stir in all your condiments. Put the pot on a medium flame. While that's coming to a boil grab a pan and brown your chop meat. Drain off the grease and add the browned meat to the pot. Cut the flame back to a minimum, cover with a lid and go watch a game. An important thing to remember here is stirring. If you have a decent pot, something with at least a double, or better yet triple base, you don't have to stir too often. These good pots will distribute the heat evenly. If you were a cheap bastard and bought a piece of shit you have to keep your eye on the bottom. Once Chili (or most anything for that matter) burns on the bottom the taste will permeate the entire pot and you might just as well dump it in Sparky's bowl. I doubt he'll even eat it. So do yourself a favor and buy a decent pot.

In one hour all the veggies will be soft and you will have Chili. It's OK Chili but... In two hours you will have good Chili. In three hours, or four hours etc.. In other words, the longer the Chili cooks the more the flavors will have a chance to meld together. Four hours is pretty much done.

Following these directions, in particular, the amount of ingredients I gave you is gonna give you a shitload of Chili. Enough for six to eight guys. Don't sweat it though if you don't eat it all. This stuff freezes so well when you defrost it next season it will taste as good as the day you made it.

*****On the day of the birth of his eleventh child the chief of the village was very upset. His first ten children were as dark in complexion as he and his wife. This eleventh child was almost white. The chief thought about it and became enraged when he figured out that the only white person in the entire village was the missionary. He found the missionary and took him to the side. "You have betrayed me", he angrily said to the missionary. "My new child is white like you." "Hold on" the missionary replied. "It can be explained. You see it's called Mendel's laws of genetics." "And what is that?" The chief asked. "Well," replied the missionary, "You see all those sheep down there. All of them but one are white. And there is one black one." "OK, OK," the chief interrupted. "You don't say nothing, I won't."

ME and THURSTON

BUFFALO WING SAUCE

If you're gonna watch games ya gotta have wings. Everybody's got their own sauce ranging from boring to molten lava. This one has a nice kick and the temp can be adjusted just by little changes in the spices. You have your purists out there who start from the very scratch. I don't, nor do most people I know. I start with a good commercial brand of hot sauce such as Frank's Hot Sauce. It's available at almost all grocery stores.
You will need:
1 quart of Frank's Hot Sauce
1 stick of butter
1/2 tsp. cayenne pepper
1/2 tsp. paprika
1/2 tap. granulated garlic
1/4 tsp. black pepper

First of all I recommend you save an empty plastic bottle with the squeeze pour top, such as a large catsup bottle. If you have left over sauce it will store nicely in this and make it easy to use. Melt the butter in a pan over a low flame. Stir in the spices. Pour this into your squeeze bottle add the Frank's and shake until the ingredients are mixed. Real rocket science, huh? The hard part, well messy part anyway is deep frying those wings. If you like wings I recommend buying one of those deep fry units like the Fry Baby or something. By the way, my favorite way to coat the wings with sauce is to put them in a plastic one gallon jug, like an empty mayo jug, squirt in the desired amount of sauce, put the lid on and shake like hell. If you know anyone in the restaurant business we throw away (I mean recycle) about twenty of those a week.

*****A blind man and his seeing eye dog are standing on the side of a busy road waiting to cross the street. The dog starts leading the man across the road into an oncoming car. The driver nails his brakes and very barely manages to avoid hitting the man. Three steps later a bicycle has to swerve and bounce off a car in order to avoid hitting the man. He curses at the man on his way by. When he was almost on the other side a taxi has to go off the road to avoid hitting him. Once safely on the other side the man reaches into his pocket and takes out a treat to give to the dog. A guy walks up to him and says, "Hey, what the hell are you rewarding that dog for. I just watched him damn near get you killed three times." "I'm not rewarding him," the blind man replied. "I'm just trying to figure out which end is which so I can kick him in the ass."

Here's the BEEF playing a little beernopoly with Noke

CLAMS ADELAIDE'S

Pretty fancy name huh? Truth is this recipe, or a reasonable facsimile to it, is an act of pure thievery. For about the last dozen years or so a couple of guys from Long Island have been regulars in my place. Whenever they're in town they stop in and we have a few. The McCabe boys, (no relation to me though I wouldn't mind if they were) run a place out on the island called Adelaide's. For twelve years I promised them I would get out to their joint. I finally did. Well it seems that the McCabe's figured they should return any generosity I might have shown them in my place. They treated me like a king and proceeded to treat me to twelve years of buy backs. Some time in the course of the night, I believe when my face started to melt, they figured they ought to get something into my belly besides tequila and beer. They brought me out some clams smothered in a sauce and some bread. As whacked as I was I still knew I was eating something mighty good. The cook brought me into the kitchen, briefly ran the ingredients by me, and sent me on my way with a jug of it. God knows I couldn't remember the recipe but a couple of days later when I sobered up I dissected it and came up with a reasonably similar flavor. McCabe's, you guys are the best and I dedicate this recipe to you.

You will need:

1 quart of half and half

1 stick of butter
1 cup of white wine
2 tbsps. of crushed garlic
1 tbsp. of chicken base
1 tsp. oregano
1 tsp. basil
1/4 tsp. pepper
1/4 cup warm water
2 tbsps. flour
As many clams as you like. (This recipe will make enough for about 8 - 10 dozen clams. It holds for a long time in the fridge)

In a large saucepan melt the butter with the wine, garlic and chicken base. Keeping the heat low stir in the half and half and the spices. Simmer this for about 10 - 12 minutes. Whisk the flour into the water and slowly whisk that mix into the sauce. Simmer for a few more minutes or until the sauce begins to thicken. Steam your clams. I'm assuming you know how to steam clams. If you don't you probably need a recipe for ice cubes too. Pour the sauce over the steamed clams saving some in a bowl for bread dipping. It's fucking outrageous! That's all I have to say about that.

*****A guy walks into a grocery store and approaches the kid working in the meat department. "I'd like to buy a Long Island duck," he says to the kid. "Sure thing," the kid replies. He goes into the back room and grabs the first duck he sees. The man takes the duck from him, tears off the plastic and sticks his thumb up the duck's ass. "Oh, you must be new here. I'm afraid you've made a mistake," the man says. "This is not a Long Island duck, this is a New Hampshire duck." "Sorry," says the kid taking the duck back. He goes into the backroom and comes out with another duck. "Yes sir, this is a Long Island duck," the kid says handing the duck to the man. Again the man peels back the plastic and sticks his thumb up the duck's ass. "Wrong again," the man says. "This is a Virginia duck." Once again the kid takes the duck back and heads for the backroom. He grabs another duck and presents it to the man. The man does the same routine. Grinning he says to the boy, "Ah, now this is a Long Island duck. Thank you very much. You are a very patient and understanding young man. Where are you from?" With that the kid turns around, drops his pants and says, "you tell me."

BARBEQUED BABY BACK RIBS

I love ribs, and I love watching people eat them. It's a beautiful thing when you can dive into a rack of ribs and not give a flying rat ass what anyone thinks of your table manners. Fuck the fork! Just give me a pile of good barbequed ribs and in five minutes I'll look like the classic picture of the one-year-old in the highchair eating his first bowl of spaghetti and sauce. Now let's not bullshit each other. Even though I will include my recipe for a good barbeque sauce I doubt you guys are really gonna bother making the sauce. Fact is there are so many great sauces out there it's hard to justify going through the time and effort of making one. In my opinion, and alot of my customers, Cattleman's Hickory smoke barbeque is great, and I dare say the best. For eight bucks you get a gallon of the stuff and that's enough sauce to do a shitload of piggies. Anyway, though the sauce is important, it's equally important how you prep your ribs. The system I'll give you here guarantees fall off the bone, melt in your mouth ribs!

You will need:

4 racks of baby back ribs

2 cups of distilled vinegar

2 cups of water

1 6oz. Can of tomato paste

Salt, pepper and garlic

Preheat the oven to 250 degrees. In a bowl mix the paste, water, vinegar and spices. In a baking pan lay out the ribs. Pour the mix over the ribs and cover the pan tightly with foil. Put the ribs in the oven and forget about them for a couple of hours. (Or if you're feeling ambitious make the sauce. Me, I'd rather go have a few brewskies.) The trick in this style of prepping the ribs is the slow cooking. Your basically steaming the ribs cooked. The vinegar in the mix breaks down the toughness of the meat and the mix just generally permeates the meat. And don't sweat if you have one too many brews and leave them in an extra 1/2 hour. It'll only make them better. After the time has passed pull the ribs. You can immediately sauce them up and throw them on the grill, stick them in the broiler or put them away for tomorrow. If you want you can make a pile and wrap them in foil and freeze them. Just take them out in time to defrost before you sauce them.

THE SAUCE

You will need:
1 cup of distilled vinegar
1 6oz. Can of tomato paste
1/3 cup of water
4 tablespoons of corn syrup
1 tbsp. of garlic powder
1 tbsp. onion powder
1 tbsp. of molasses
1 tbsp. of liquid smoke flavor
2 tsps. of sugar
1/4 tsp. pepper

There's no secret to this. Just dump everything in a pot and let it simmer for about 15 minutes. That's it.

***** A blonde chick was so disgusted with the abuse she took for being a blonde she dyes her hair brunette. Feeling quite happy with the change and the expected respect she would receive she decides to take a ride through the country. She comes across a sheep farm and pulls over to look at the cute little animals. The farmer sees her and walks over to her. "Can I help you miss," the farmer asks. "Why yes," the blonde says. "They're so cute. If I can guess how many are there can I have one of the little cute ones?" "Sure," the farmer replied, "take a guess." "157," the blonde guesses. "Why, that's amazing!" the farmer replied. "There are exactly 157 sheep there." With that the excited blonde runs into the field and makes her choice. As she's getting into her car with her new pet the farmer asks her, "Hey lady, if I can guess the real color of your hair can I have my dog back?"

BIG TIM, PATTY, ME, PAULY "MON", JUDY AND ALLEN on PAULY "MON"S big day.

SANDWICHES

GRILLED CHICKEN WRAP

Wraps are cool. They'd like you to believe that these things originated somewhere out in California by some health freaks. At least that's what Californians want you to think. Truth is, given the proximity to Mexico, I think it's just a variation on a theme, so to speak. Mexican's have been putting everything under the sun in tortilla shells since just slightly after the Stone Age. And that's all wraps are. A big ole tortilla shell, some corn, some flour and an endless variety of flavored ones, stuffed with whatever you feel like putting in them. I'll throw a couple of ideas at you and from there you run with it. One of my favorites is the grilled chicken wrap. You will need:

12 inch tortilla shells (You pick the flavor)

4 skinned and boned chicken breasts

1 good sized tomato (like c-cup size)

1/2 cup of fresh scallions. (You'll have to buy one bunch. That's just the way they come. You could substitute onion but the strength of the taste of onions might overpower everything else.)

Chicken seasoning. (Available at most any store. I should have listed this and steak seasoning in the list I made of must have spices.)

1/2 lb. bacon (roughly eight to ten strips)

1 stick of Monterey Jack cheese

1/2 cup ranch dressing
Cooking oil

Slice your chicken into 1/2-inch strips.
Coat the bottom of a frying pan with oil. Put the pan over a medium flame. When the oil is good and hot put your chicken strips in the pan and give them a good coating of chicken seasoning. Get the bacon cooking too.
While the chicken and bacon are cooking, dice up the tomatoes and scallions. Grate up a pile of the cheese.
Lay out your tortillas and put a nice bead of cheese down the center. When the chicken and bacon are done put two strips of bacon and as much chicken as you like on the cheese in the tortilla. Put some tomatoes and scallions in each shell and ladle some ranch over the whole shebang. Tuck the sides in and roll her up. That's it, you're done. The beauty of this recipe is that there is no particular amount of any of the ingredients. You like more chicken, you put more chicken in. More tomatoes, less tomatoes,

it doesn't matter. Have it your way! I usually get about six wraps out of the ingredients I listed here.

*****A gorilla is walking through the jungle one afternoon and he comes across a lion with his entire head and mane tangled in a briar patch struggling desperately to get free. The gorilla watches for a while and realizes the lion has no chance of getting free. "Well, look here" he says, "the mighty king of the jungle." The gorilla decides to take advantage of the situation and has his way with the lion. When he's done he leaves and is chuckling to himself as he walks away. The lion was so furious that he, the mighty king of the jungle, had just been violated by a lowly gorilla. With a renewed strength he breaks away and starts charging looking to kill the gorilla. When the gorilla hears the lion's roars getting louder he realizes that he is free and coming for him. He starts running searching desperately for a place to hide. He comes upon a tent in an encampment. Just before the lion is upon him he grabs a jacket and hat and puts them on. He takes a seat and picks up a newspaper and pretends to be reading. He no sooner has the paper over his face and the lion comes bursting into the tent. "Has anyone here seen a gorilla recently?" He roars. "Do you mean the one who fucked the lion in the ass?" Asks the gorilla nervously. "Christ, don't tell me it's in the paper already", the lion replied.

STEAK WRAP

I've got more wraps than P. Diddy or M & M or whoever the fuck those guys are. Anyway, I'm just gonna throw a few at you in this book. I'm sure you'll come up with your own.

You will need:

4 Tortilla shells
1 lb. beef - top round or sirloin are best
1 medium onion
1 bell pepper
1 tomato
8 oz. whatever cheese you like
Steak seasoning
Cooking oil

 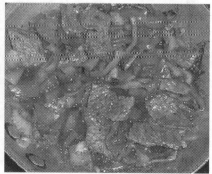

Coat a good sized pan with oil. Slice your steak into 1/4 inch strips. Julienne cut the onion and pepper. Put them in the pan and cook them until they are soft. Add the sliced steak and give it a good shake of steak seasoning. Cook to the way you like your steak; i.e. medium, rare, well, etc... Dice the tomato and add to the pan just before the steak is done cooking. (Just to warm it up.) Divide your steak into the center of the wraps and grate the cheese onto it. Roll it up and serve.

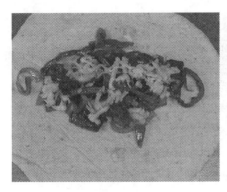 

*****At the turn of the century an Irishman, O'Reilly, immigrates to the U.S. Soon after arriving he decides that he must go see a baseball game since he had heard so much about it. He gets himself a good seat by the field. In the first inning the first man up slaps a line drive down third base line. "Run, run," everyone jumps to their feet and starts yelling. The batter drops his bat and takes off running. The next man up drops a short fly ball into a hole in midfield. "Run, run," everyone is yelling. O'Reilly joins them in the chant. When the third man gets a hit O'Reilly is well into the spirit of the game screaming at the top of his lungs. When the fourth player is walked he drops his bat and slowly jogs out to first base. Enraged by the player's lack of enthusiasm O'Reilly jumps up and yells, "Run you lazy bastard!" With that the man next to him turns and says, "He can't run, he's got four balls." Hearing this O'Reilly stands and shouts, "Walk proudly son!"

Summer Day Next Door At WAREHOUSE III

CUBAN SANDWICH

I don't know what the origin of this sandwich is or for that matter why it's called a Cuban. Some chick made it for me once and when I asked her what it was she said a Cuban. I'd like to give her credit for this sandwich but although I can remember the name of the sandwich, I can't remember hers. This dish is great for parties or can be a dinner.

You will need: (for 4)

1/2 to 3/4 lbs of ham or pastrami (depending on how much meat you like)

4 hoagie rolls

1/4 lb. Swiss cheese

1 10oz. can sauerkraut

thousand island dressing

butter

Heat the sauerkraut in a pot. Slice the rolls length wise. Cut the hump off the top of the roll. Spread some thousand island dressing on both sides of the roll. Melt a couple of slices of butter in a pan. When the sauerkraut is hot, place the ham (or pastrami), cheese, and sauerkraut evenly on the roll. Put them in the pan and press them as flat as you can. (I don't know why but for some reason they taste better flattened out.) When it's browned on one side turn it over and brown the other. This is a great sandwich. Like I said, I can remember the name of the sandwich.....

*****A shy guy is sitting in a crowded bar alone watching everyone have a good time. He notices a woman who is also sitting alone and musters up enough balls to go over and talk to her. " Hi," he says "mind if I sit here with you and perhaps buy you a drink?" With that the woman stands up and shouts at the top of her lungs, "No! I will not have sex with you!" Everybody in the place is staring at the guy. The poor guy is so embarrassed he slithers back over to his seat alone. A few minutes later the same woman comes over to him and says, "Look, I'm really sorry. You see I'm a psychology student and I was just doing an experiment to see how people react to adverse conditions." With that the guys stands up and yells, "You want how much!"

PHILLY CHEESE STEAK

I don't know why Philly was given the honor of having this sandwich named after them. I've been eating them for as long as I can remember down on the boardwalk in Jersey. Anyway, there's a reason why every fair, carnival or festival sells billions of these. Hell, you can't swing a dead cat in Seaside Heights without hitting a Cheese steak stand. It's a great sandwich, and fast and easy to make.

You will need:
1 lb. top round steak
1 bell pepper
1 medium onion
1/4 lb. American cheese
4 hoagie rolls
Steak seasoning
Cooking oil

Before you even start this recipe I must tell you if you try to get lazy and make this sandwich with Steak-um's or any other of those processed meat products I will hunt you down and beat you with a claw hammer. There is no substitute for the real top round steak. Ok, now that we're all on the same page, let's start. Lightly coat the bottom of a large frying pan with oil and put over a medium heat. Julienne cut the onion and pepper and sauté them until they are soft. Not burnt, just soft. While that's going on slice the steak as thin as you can. When the veggies are done take them off and keep them warm. (Do not drain the oil) Actually, just putting them in a bowl will keep them warm enough. In the same pan lay the steak out, sprinkle a bit of steak seasoning over it and cook to your desired wellness. Slice the hoagie rolls lengthwise. Portion the steak in the pan into as many portions as you like. Place three slices of cheese across the top of each steak portion. Place the open hoagie rolls over the top of each portion to melt the cheese. (About one minute.) When the cheese is melted place one hand on top of the roll and a spatula under the meat and flip it over. This may take some practice. Add the peppers and onions, as you like.

*****Q. What's the difference between a lawyer and a catfish?

      A One is a bottom dwelling scum sucker and the
                other is a fish.

CHICKEN TERIYAKI

This dish makes a good dinner when served with rice, but it also makes a damn good sandwich. It's basically just a grilled chicken sandwich. The Teriyaki Sauce is the secret.
You will need:
4 chicken breasts boned and skinned
1/4 lb. Swiss cheese
The sauce:
1/2 cup soy sauce
1/4 cup cooking oil
1/2 cup honey
3 tsps. crushed garlic
1/2 tsp. salt
1/4 tsp. pepper
1/2 tsp. ginger.

It's best to make this sauce ahead of time. When I make it at the restaurant I quadruple the recipe and keep it in an empty vodka bottle. It has a great shelf life and does not need to be refrigerated. In any event, all the ingredients go into a bottle and just shake the shit out of it. The ingredients separate very quickly so always shake before using.

Pound the breasts down to 1/2 inch thickness. Coat

the bottom of a frying pan with the teri sauce and put on a medium flame. Stab the breasts a few times with a fork and pour a little more sauce on them. Cover the pan with a lid and let them cook for about five minutes. Turn them over and continue cooking. From start to finish should only be ten minutes. When they are done, put a layer of Swiss cheese over each and cover until the cheese melts. About one more minute.

*****Bill Clinton was un-boarding Air Force 1 on return from a peace keeping effort in China. Under each arm he had a pot-bellied pig, a gift from the Chinese embassy. The usual entourage of secret service men were there to greet him. As he walked by one agent remarked, "They're very cute Sir." "Thanks," Bill said. "I got them for Hillary." "Good trade Sir," the agent replied.

DINNER TIME

MEATLOAF

Meatloaf is one of my favorites. It's so easy to make yet I've tasted some real bricks in my time. This loaf should take you about ten minutes to put together.
You will need:
3 lbs chop meat *(85/15 is best. Not too fatty but enough to give you a juicy loaf)
4 large eggs
1 medium sized onion
1 1/2 cups of bread crumbs
1 tsp. salt
1/2 tsp. pepper
1 tbsp. crushed garlic
1/2 cup warm water
1tsp. beef base
1tbsp. steak seasoning

Ready, here we go.
1. Dice your onion
2. Mix the beef base with the water
3. Dump everything in a bowl and mash it together with your hands. NO spoon, it takes too long.
Now get yourself a pan and mold it together to look like whatever you like. Perhaps a car or fish or a nice set of boobs. The main thing is to make sure the loaf is about three to four inches high so it doesn't dry out. Cover your pan with foil and bake at 425 for forty-five minutes. Take the foil off and bake for another fifteen minutes. This will give the loaf a nice crisp and brown finish.

*85/15 refers to the fat content in the meat. The higher the first number the leaner the meat.

*****A guy is out in the woods hunting when he spots a bear and takes a shot at him. Unfortunately, he misses the bear. The enraged bear charges the guy and grabs him by the collar. " You just tried to kill me," the bear says. "In all fairness I should rip you to shreds. But instead I'll make you a deal. You get on your knees and do the right thing and I'll let you live." The man begrudgingly performs the necessary act to save his life. " Now get out of my woods," the bear says, "or I might kill you yet."

Once in the safety of his cabin the man is overcome with anger and makes a plan to kill the bear. For the next few days he stalks the bear and learns his every move. When the time was right he took his best shot at the bear. Unfortunately, he misses again. He tries to run for safety but the bear catches him. "You again," the bear growled. "You know what to do." Once again the man performs the nasty act and the bear lets him go. Now the man was so furious that he went and bought the best equipment money could buy. With a long-range rifle and a powerful scope he set out to kill the bear. When he spotted him he took his best shot. He started walking towards the spot feeling certain he had made his kill. When he got there he couldn't find the bear. He felt a tap on his shoulder and when he turned around it was the bear. The bear looked at him and said, "You don't really come here to hunt, do you?"

Bar top dancin' at the Warehouse

CHICKEN PARMESAN

This is one of those dishes that, although still relatively easy to make, have a couple of steps involved; therefore you may have to turn the television towards you. Just a bit more time involved, but hell, you've been eating that Chili for three days now. It's time to move on. The beauty of this dish is that it's one more thing to do with that left over sauce you made. If you don't have any leftover sauce, well, I guess you're in for some time.

You will need:

4 chicken breasts skinned and boned (if you buy the full breasts you will have to split them and trim them yourself, you cheap bastard. I recommend buying them already trimmed and split by the butcher. For a few cents more it's faster and easier.)

1 cup of flour

1 egg

1/4 cup of milk

1/4 cup of cooking oil

1/4 cup of Parmesan Cheese

1 lb of mozzarella

1/4 tsp. salt and pepper

Preheat oven to 350 degrees

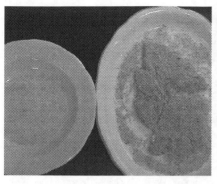

Lay out a piece of plastic wrap on the cutting board, place a breast on it and cover it with another piece of plastic. Find a suitable tool such as a mallet, rolling pin or an anvil. Step back and think of that last person who really needed to have the living shit choked out of them. Now, with that in mind pound that breast down to about 1/4 inch thickness. Feels good huh? Who says cooking ain't fun? Now whip the milk and egg together in a bowl. Next, add the salt and pepper to the flour and mix dry. Place the flour on a plate. Put some oil in a frying pan and put a medium flame under it. When the oil is hot, don't burn it, dip each piece of chicken in the egg, then the flour and fry it to a nice golden brown in the oil. Do not over-cook it or you will have chicken jerky. Remember, this is going to go in the oven as well so if it's slightly under cooked don't sweat it. It will finish cooking in the oven. When all your chicken is browned get a baking dish, coat it with oil and lay your chicken out in it. Cover generously with your sauce. Sprinkle the

Parmesan cheese over the chicks and cover each piece with a slice of Mozzarella. Bake in the oven at 350 degrees for 20 - 30 minutes or until browned. When you serve it, a nice touch is to ladle a bit of sauce over it.

*****Three gals, a blonde, brunette, and a redhead decide they are going to make a living robbing warehouses. On their first attempt they set off an alarm bringing the police almost immediately. They run to the back of the warehouse and find a pile of sacks. They each find an empty one and climb in and hide themselves amongst the pile. An officer walks by and kicks the sack the brunette is in. "Meow", he hears, and figuring it was just a cat moves along. He comes to the sack the redhead is in and gives it a kick. "Woof", he hears, and figuring it's just a dog he moves along. He gets to the sack the blonde is in and gives it a kick. "Potato" he hears.

POT ROAST

This is a great meal. Nothin' to it, prep time is about ten to fifteen minutes and everybody loves pot roast. Seriously, you could teach a monkey to cook this. You will need:

1 2 - 3 lb. piece of bottom round beef (Look for a flat cut. It usually says "Flat cut" on the label)
6 - 8 medium sized potatoes
2 large onions
8 or so carrots
Salt, pepper and granulated garlic
Set oven at 325 degrees

Wash the potatoes and cut them into quarters. Don't bother peeling them unless you have a thing against potato skins. They'll be so tender you won't even notice them anyway. Wash the carrots and cut them into 1/2-inch slices. Same rule about peeling. Julienne cut the onions. OK, these ya wanna peel. Now get a roasting pot with enough room to put your beef and all this other stuff in. After everybody's in the boat pour about one and a half inches of water in. Lightly cover everything with salt, pepper and garlic. Don't go too heavy. Remember you can always add more, but it's a bitch to take off. Now cover your pot tightly with foil and put it in the oven. With a tight cover and 325 degrees you're going to get a nice slow even steam cook. Like I said the prep time is only 10 - 15 minutes. Cooking time is about two hours. So have something to do while it's cooking. You could mow the lawn, or paint the house or get a six-pack and watch sports center. At any rate, in two hours you have a complete meal.

*By the way, all that juice in the bottom of the pan makes an excellent gravy. Mix about 2 tbsps. of flour with warm water, put the juice and flour mixture in a pot and over a low flame stir until it thickens.

*****A guy is out shooting a round of golf. He hits the best drive of his life right into the foursome ahead of him. He's sees a guy drop his club, grab his leg and start hopping around obviously in pain. Realizing his ball hit the guy he jumps in his cart and hurries up to apologize to the man. When he gets there the injured man hollers at him "you idiot, I'm a lawyer and I could sue you for five thousand dollars." "For Christ's sake'" the man replied, "I yelled fore." "All right, fours good" replied the lawyer.

MEATBALLS

I love meatballs. I love meatballs with pasta, meatball parmesan heroes, meatballs all by themselves. They're even great for a cold sandwich. I've had lots of meatballs made by lots of different people. Almost all are good, although different. Without a doubt, the best I've ever had were made by the old Italian guys in my old neighborhood. I stole their recipes many years ago and have made just a few changes to suit my taste.

You will need:

2 lbs. of ground beef (85/15 will do)

3 large or x-tra large eggs

3 tbsp chopped garlic

2 tbsp. basil

2 tbsp. parsley

2 tbsp oregano

1 & 1/2 cup of breadcrumbs

1 large, not gigantic onion (about the size of a hardball)

1/2 cup of milk

1 tsp. salt

pinch of pepper

oil (for frying the meatballs)

Finely dice your onion. In a mixing bowl add all your ingredients. Mix all that stuff around until it looks like everything is mixed evenly throughout. Now roll the mix into little balls about the size of a racquetball. That's slightly larger than a golf ball and just under a, hell, I don't know. About 2 inches in diameter. You know what two inches looks like. Think swimming in cold water.

Coat the bottom of a good-sized pan with oil. When the oil is hot start dropping your balls in it. Are we having fun yet? Keep rolling the balls around so they cook on all sides. (Spheres don't have sides, do they?) Hey if you're not gonna put these in sauce, which would be silly, just break one open to see if they're done. If you are adding these to sauce keep them a tad on the rare side. Let the sauce finish cooking them. This way they stay nice and soft. The tomato sauce at the beginning of this book is the perfect bath for these bad boys. Let them simmer in there for an hour or more. Bon Appetit!

*****One night a ventriloquist was doing his act in a small town. He was having a good time doing his usual routine of blonde jokes when suddenly a large blonde chick jumps up on her stool and interrupts him. " All right pal," the blonde shouts. "I've had enough of you degrading women just because of the color of their hair. The stereotyping is overplayed and ridiculous. It's because of assholes like you that I can't go any further in my job. You know, I have a half a mind to come up there and kick the shit out of you." The startled ventriloquist starts to apologize to the blonde. "Ma'am, I'm really sorry I..." The blonde cuts him off. "You stay out of this; I'm talking to the little fucker on your knee."

QUESADILLAS

Ten years ago nine out of ten people never heard of quesadillas, never mind pronounce it. By the way, it is pronounced "Case a d ass", as in I got a case a de ass. Whatever that means; but it's a good way to remember it. So anyway, these days everyone knows what they are and probably most have tried one. This is another beauty dish from our south of the boarder brothers who taught us how to pronounce sinsemilla. I'll give you the basic, and from there you can run with it. Christ, this is so easy I feel stupid even printing it. But, and this is a big but, it's so damn pretty on the plate and it is delicious, that you're bound to get a little just for presentation alone.
You will need: (for four)
4 tortilla shells - 8 inchers are best but since they come in a variety of sizes you make the call. Another thing that you should know is that they usually come 12 in a pack. It's cool though cause they freeze nicely.
12 oz bar of cheese. Any kind you like. Most places serve them with cheddar or muenster. I use both. Or if you want a little heat try a pepper cheese.
1 tomato
1 head of lettuce (not even, but they don't sell half heads; which reminds me of a good joke.)
1 pint of sour cream
1bag of tortilla chips
Salsa (optional)

Lay out the tortilla shells on the counter. Grate enough cheese to cover 1/2 of each shell. Fold the top over and place them in a large skillet or pan over a low flame. Dice your tomato and thin slice your lettuce. When the cheese starts to get soft, which should only be about two minutes, turn them over. Pay attention cause they burn easily. Two more minutes on that side and you are done. Cut them into four wedges and put them on one side of the plate. On the other side of the plate put some tomatoes on one side and lettuce on the other. In the middle put some chips. The salsa is for the chips. I like to put some on my quesadilla. Put a dollop of sour cream on any available spot on the plate. Done. Pretty, ain't it? I know I've been blabbing here for a while but in reality you can make this dish faster than you can write it.

A good time to make quesadillas is when you have some leftovers hanging around the fridge. If you have some left over chicken, tear it into little pieces, put it in a pan with some butter and cumin, heat it up and add it to the cheese. It works with damn near anything. My friend Junior, owner of Rattlesnake Jake's in Deerfield Beach, Fla. made me some Amberjack (that's a fish you damn land lovers) Quesadillas that knocked me out. Thank you Junior. Hey Junior! I figured out how you could sell twice as much beer. Try filling the mugs up.

*****An extremely large scary looking man walks up to the kid working the produce stand. "I'd like to buy a half a head of lettuce", the large man says. "One minute," the kid says, "I'll be right back." The kid walks to the back of the store, pushes the door open and hollers to his friend. "You're not gonna believe this, some asshole out there wants to buy a half a head of lettuce." He looks to his right and the angry man is standing right there. "And this gentleman would like to buy the other half," he adds.

ROAST PORK TENDERLOIN

Pork, the other white meat (as they call it), is a nice change from beef or chicken. It used to be that pork was the pricey stuff but these days you can catch it on sale for less than a lot of cuts of beef or chicken. The only problem with pork tenderloin is that unless you buy the whole tenderloin, which is where the bargain is, they're gonna stick it right up the ole wazul when you buy it. The whole loin can go up to 10 - 12 lbs. That's a lot of pork if you're just cooking for two to six people. If you buy what the stores call pork medallions, it gets expensive. Don't let any one b.s. you. A medallion is just a slice off a whole loin. Me, I say buy the whole loin, slice off what you need and freeze the rest. Same as freezing beef or chicken.

You will need:

1 pork tenderloin
Salt, pepper, garlic powder and paprika

Preheat your oven to 325. Place the loin, fat side down, in a baking pan. Lightly sprinkle all your spices over the top. Pour 1/2 cup water on the bottom of the tray. Cover the pan tightly with foil. The tight foil combined with the low temperature and the water will steam the loin making it very tender. Put it in the oven for 1 & 1/2 hours. Remove the foil and let it get nice and browned. It's about another 15 - 30 minutes. If you have a meat thermometer 160 degrees is done. This dish is so easy to make and I swear you can't screw it up. The only problem is that from time of prep to time of serve is a couple of hours. I recommend putting it in the oven at the end of the first quarter.

*****A woman and her lover were going at it hot and heavy when they hear her husband's car pulling into the driveway. The lover grabs his clothes and hides in the closet as the woman throws on some clothes to go downstairs to head her husband off. "Boy, sure is dark in here," the man hears. His eyes adjust to the light and he sees the woman's son sitting there. "Shhh," the man says. "Wanna buy my baseball?" the kid says. "Yeah sure," the man replies just to shut the kid up. "How much?" "Fifty dollars," the kid replies. The man reluctantly pays the hush money to the kid, gets dressed and sneaks out the window. Two weeks later while the woman and her lover were going at it the husband again shows up unexpectedly. The lover again jumps into the closet. "Sure is dark in here," the kid says. "How much?" the man asks wearily. "I'll give you my glove for $100," the kid says. Again the man pays up and leaves. A few nights later the father comes home from work and asks the kid to go have a catch. The kid tells the father he no longer has a ball or glove. He tells his dad that he sold them to a friend for $150. "Why that's a sin charging your friend so much money for that ball and glove. I want you to go to confession and tell the priest what you've done," the father scolded. The next day the kid goes to the church and into the confessional. "Sure is dark in here," the kid says. "You're not gonna start that shit again," the priest replied.

MOM, MAURICE,(the king of cool) ME, AUNT PEG, MAUREEN. They don't make them like that anymore.

EGGPLANT PARMESAN

Here's yet another one of those "Parmesan" dishes. You got your chicken, veal, and now eggplant. The thing that sets eggplant Parmesan apart is that it is a meat free dish. You can't call it vegetarian because it does contain cheese. It's fast and easy to make especially if you have your sauce already made. If not, well, a few more minutes.

You will need: (approximately 6 - 8 servings.)

2 medium sized eggplants (to determine medium size hold up a small one next to a large one and get something in between)

3 cups of breadcrumbs (seasoned)

4 eggs

1/2 cup milk

1/2 cup Parmesan cheese

1 lb sliced Mozzarella

Tomato Sauce

Olive oil

Salt, pepper, oregano

Preheat the oven to 325 degrees. In a bowl mix the eggs and milk with a dash of pepper and a couple of dashes of salt. Lay out about a cup of breadcrumbs on a plate. Now here's where "traditional" and "my way" take separate paths. In the old neighborhood they never peeled the eggplant. I peel mine. After all, cooked eggplant is a very tender dish. Who needs this purple shoelace (the peel) interfering with a nice tender slice of eggplant? Take my word, it doesn't chew well. Anyway, peel the eggplant and slice it into 1/2 discs. Take your slices and dip them into the egg mix and directly coat them with breadcrumbs. Just lay them on the crumbs and turn them over. Coat the bottom of a good-sized frying pan with oil and put a medium flame under it. Fry your slices till they're a nice golden brown. Coat the bottom of a baking dish with oil and lay your cooked slices in the tray. Just one layer. Sprinkle a little oregano on the slices then do the same with the Parmesan cheese. Now pour sauce over the top and put a slice of mozzarella over the layer.

Repeat for the next layer and the next. Don't go over three high cause it'll fall apart when you go to serve it. That would suck after all that work. Though it would taste the same, serving something that looks like it was already chewed does not impress.

*****A guy is walking down the beach when he comes across an odd looking lamp. He bends down and picks up the lamp, and as always, gives it a rub. Sure enough out comes a genie. "I can grant you one, and only one wish", the genie says. "Well," says the guy, "I've always wanted to go to Hawaii but I'm scared to death of flying and even more scared of being out in that big ocean on a boat. I would like you to build me a bridge across the ocean so I can drive there." "Hold on there" the genie says. "I can do most anything but that is kinda stretching the limit of what even I can do. I'll tell you what, I'll give you another wish." "Hmm," the man says. "Alright, I've got one. My wife and I don't get along. She cut me off from sex about 20 years ago. I want you to make me irresistible to her. I want her to attack me sexually morning, noon and night." The genie replies, " So how many lanes you want on that bridge?"

Yes there really is an International Organization called the "Old Bastards". That's me with our local chapter president, BIG JOHN

SLOPPY JOES

Sloppy Joe's, ah yes! The name alone conjures up images of those glorious days gone by. Mrs. Condalucie, the ninety-four year old lunch lady who would pile generous mounds of the slop upon a fresh burger roll. Sloppy Joe day was right up there with Salisbury steak day. Some recipes are timeless. This is one of them.

You will need: (4 - 6 servings)

1lb. chop meat
1 small onion (real small)
1 small bell pepper (same deal)
1- 6 oz. can of tomato paste
1 pack of burger rolls
1 cup of catsup
1 tsp. garlic
1/2 tsp. salt
1 tsp paprika
1 tsp. chile powder
1/4 tsp. pepper
splash of cooking oil

In one pan brown your burger meat. Dice up, real fine, your pepper and onion. Put some oil in another pan and lightly cook your onions and peppers. Just enough to make them soft. When the burger is browned, drain the fat. Now add everything else to the burger meat plus about 1& 1/2 cup of water and the catsup. Turn you flame down real low and let the dish simmer till it tightens up. About 15 - 20 minutes. Pile it on a roll and there you go. Class dismissed!

*****A pilot gets on the loud speaker shortly after take off. "Folks, welcome to flight 314 nonstop to N.Y. We'll be cruising at thirty thousand feet and it looks like it's gonna be smooth sailing all the way. So kick back, take off your shoes, relax, and enjoy the flight." He forgets to turn the mike off and turns to the co-pilot and says, "Listen, you take over for a while. I'm gonna go take me a big ole healthy shit and then I'm gonna fuck the brains outta that cute little stewardess in coach." His voice is heard over the whole plane. The stewardess panics. "Oh my God", she says and starts running to the front of the plane. An old lady sitting in an aisle seat stops her and says, "Relax honey, he's gotta take a shit first".

PAULY MON'S PARTY

LEMON GARLIC CHICKEN

This is another one of those chicken dishes that is relatively quick and easy to prepare. What is nice about this dish is that it is not something you have everyday and it looks like you actually put a whole lot of thought and effort into it.

You will need:

4 chicken breasts boned and skinned
1 lemon
1 tbsp. chopped garlic
1 cup of flour
1/2 tsp. granulated garlic
1 tsp. salt
1/4 tsp pepper
1 cup wine
1/4 cup chopped scallions
1 tbsp. chicken base
cooking oil

Place the breasts between plastic and pound them down to 1/4 to 1/2-inch thickness. Cut the breasts into 1-inch strips. Add the salt, pepper and granulated garlic to the flour dry. Mix it up good. Coat the bottom of a frying pan with oil and put it on a medium heat. Roll the strips of chicken in the flour mix until they are lightly coated and fry them in the oil. Cook for about 3 - 4 minutes or until golden brown. If your oil starts smoking it is too hot! Dump that oil and start with fresh or you'll ruin everything. Anyway, assuming that you have not burned the oil, continue on until all the strips are done. Put the cooked strips aside. Preferably somewhere they will stay warm. Now in that same pan add your wine, garlic, scallions, chicken base and as much juice as you can squeeze out of that lemon. Oh yeah, cut the lemon in quarters for maximum juiceage. Stir it up good and bring to a boil. Now take the remaining flour mix, (no more than two tablespoons) and mix it with some lukewarm water until you get a paste. Turn your flame down to a simmer and whisk in the flour paste. Add your cooked chicken roll it around for another minute or two and you're done. You can serve this over just about anything. Hell you could pour it over some greens and have a salad. Call it anything you like as long as you use California in the name. Like, California Lemon Chicken Salad. God you're a genius!

*****In a posh restaurant a stuffy waiter walks up to a man who has just finished his entree. "How did you find your steak Sir?" the waiter asked. The man replied, "Quite accidentally. I moved the tomato."

Groucho Marx

BEEF TIPS AND BROCCOLI

This is a dish I make whenever I have leftover beef. It doesn't necessarily have to be made with leftovers but it beats wasting food. Let's say you invite a half a dozen guys over for beer and horseshoes. You pick up two big ole London broils, marinate them for a day or so and toss them on the grill. It comes time to eat and two guys are passed out on lawn chairs, three guys are too drunk to actually comprehend the function of getting anything but beer to their lips and one guy keeps sneaking off to the corner and for some unknown reason the thought of eating seems to nauseate him. I have seen this happen once or twelve times. Anyway, the next day you have a slab of London broil left and everyone has gone home. You could make sliced London broil sandwiches for the next week. But since your old lady is probably pissed at you for some silly thing like your buddies used her prized flower garden for a urinal, you might want to consider making her a nice dinner and letting her keep the nickels from the beer can deposits.
You will need:
1 lb. beef (if it's a leftover and has already been cooked, great. If not the cooking time will just be a bit longer.)
1 large onion
1 large head of broccoli
1 tbsp. crushed garlic

1 tbsp. beef base
1/2 tsp. salt
1/4 tsp. pepper
2 quarts of water (for cooked beef. add 1/2 more for uncooked)

* If you're starting with uncooked beef put your water in a pot and get it boiling. Cut your beef into one inch cubes and put them in the boiling water. Let them roll around in the boiling water until they are cooked. About 15 to 20 minutes. DO NOT dump this water. It will be the water used in this recipe. Now follow the rest of the recipe as if you were starting with cooked beef. Cut your beef into one-inch cubes. Julienne cut your onions. Put your water, beef and everything else except the broccoli into the water and get it boiling. Keep it on a high boil for about 45 minutes. A good bit of your water will boil away. That's what we want to happen. Don't let it go dry. If you need to, add a little more water. Cut your broccoli into little heads. Pick out a piece of beef and taste it to see if it's nice and tender. It should be by now. If not let it boil a little longer. When it is tender toss your broccoli in and let it cook for about five minutes. We want the broc to stay firm. Serve this dish over rice with flowers. Now go have a hair of the dog that bit you. *Most any cut of beef will work in this recipe. I've even used prime rib. Just not ground beef you knucklehead.

*****An older nun and a younger nun were riding their bicycle built for two back to the convent on some old back roads. "Sister," the younger nun in the rear said, "I don't believe I've ever come this way before." The older nun replied, "It's the cobblestones honey."

SHRIMP SCAMPI

If you like seafood this is one of the easiest and tastiest recipes around. You know it's easy because when you go into a restaurant that has a limited seafood selection shrimp scampi is always there. You can make this dish with fresh shrimp or with frozen depending on how much time you want to spend. If you go with fresh you'll have to peel and de-vein the shrimp. It's time consuming. If you go with frozen buy the UNCOOKED C.P.D.; which means cleaned, peeled and de veined. Unless you go to a restaurant that is primarily seafood, or charges $60 a plate you are more than likely eating frozen shrimp. Fact is there are so many strong flavors in this recipe I'll be dipped in shit and rolled in popcorn if I can tell the difference. So let's go with frozen for now. Just throw the bag away. You don't have to tell her it was frozen.

You will need:

2lbs. *16 - 24 shrimp (that's how many shrimp per pound)

1 stick of butter

1 lemon

1 cup of white wine

1/4 cup chopped parsley

1/2 tsp. salt

1/4 tsp pepper

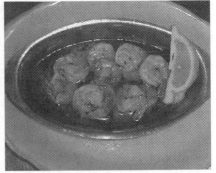

Get your shrimp ahead of time so it's defrosted at time of cooking. In a pan melt 1/2 stick of butter and add the shrimp. Roll the shrimp around until they are cooked, i.e. no longer transparent. It's just a few minutes. Any longer will make them chewy. When they are cooked put them aside. In the same pan add the rest of the butter and everything else. (Don't throw the whole lemon in, squeeze about 1 & 1/2 tbsp. of juice in.) Stir it around until the flavors are blended, which is about 4 - 5 minutes. Put the shrimp back in the pan and stir for about 1 - 2 minutes. That's it. Serve it over rice or angel hair pasta or Alpo if you choose.

* The above recipe is a clear sauce scampi. If you would like some texture to your sauce just blend 1 tbsp. of flour with 1/4 cup of wine and stir in before you add the shrimp.

*****Two six year old boys were walking home from school. One turns to the other and says, "Last night I found a used condom on my patio." The other kid asks, "What's a patio?"

BIG MAX, MARLENA, DAN, SLY, JODIE, ME

Every year on Thanksgiving we open our doors to feed the hungry. Each year we have different volunteers for the grueling task. (It's only grueling because the biggest party day of the year at McCabe's is the day before.) All the customers donate the food and clothing. I like to call it "Soul Masturbation."

BAKED ZITI

I like this recipe for its simplicity. If you haven't noticed by now, I like a lot of recipes for that reason. Seems like everybody likes ziti. It's another one of those dishes that can be made meatless. This is also another one of those recipes that's real easy if you happen to have a sauce already made. If not, be a sport. Go on, make the sauce. Just make enough so you have some left to freeze for the next recipe.

You will need:

1lb. Uncooked ziti
1 qt. sauce (meat or meatless)
1 lb. ricotta cheese
1lb. Mozzarella cheese
4 tbsp. grated Parmesan cheese
1tbsp. Parsley flakes, oregano and garlic powder
1/2 tsp. salt
1/4 tsp. pepper
2 tbsp. oil

In a good-sized pot boil about 6 quarts of water with the oil. Add the ziti and cook. Again, like most pasta, don't overcook it. Put your sauce on a low flame, just enough to warm it up. In a bowl mix your ricotta, Parmesan and all your spices. Now add about three cups of your sauce and the cooked, (drained) ziti and continue mixing. Pour your mix into a baking tray and spread it evenly. Pour the remaining sauce over the top evenly. Slice the mozzarella and cover the whole deal evenly. Cover with foil and bake at 350 degrees for 30 minutes or until the cheese is nicely melted. And that's all I have to say about that!

*****An eight year old boy is sitting in his backyard when he sees a stray dog humping his neighbor's dog. He runs into the house shouting "Mommy, come quick! Some big dog is beating up on the Smith's dog." His mom comes out of the house and upon seeing what is happening calmly explains to her son, "No honey, he's not beating her up. They're just making puppies." Two weeks later the kid is awakened by the love making moans coming from his parent's bedroom. He runs to their door to find his father on top of mom pounding away. Shocked, he yells, "Stop daddy, you're hurting mommy!" His father stops and calmly turns to his son and says, "Daddy wouldn't hurt mommy, we're just making you a little brother. "Heck dad," says the kid, "turn her over. I want a puppy."

SALISBURY STEAK

"What could possibly be wrong children? It's Salisbury Steak day." Chef of South Park.

What a great line, one of my favorites, from a great show. The greatness in that line is how short and sweet it is yet it threw me back to fourth grade lunch. Salisbury steak day was just about the best. Man when I'd hear that it was Salisbury steak day my stomach would start rumbling. I could eat three of those things with no problem. I'd trade away lunches, desserts, money, and even baseball cards to get them. Alas, I must admit, I would even flirt with the lunch lady to get seconds. And it's still a favorite. When I put it on my lunch special at the tavern it always sells out. Call it a glorified hamburger or a mini meatloaf. It doesn't matter. Just hurry up and make them.

You will need:

2 lbs. of chop meat

1 medium onion

4 eggs

1/2 cup of milk

2 tbsp. parsley flakes

1 tsp. salt

1/4 tsp pepper

Preheat the oven to 350 degrees.

Finely dice the onion. Mix everything in a bowl. Lightly oil the bottom of a baking pan. Shape the mix into 6" x 4" loaves. Put them in the pan and cover tightly. Bake for 40 minutes. Make the onion gravy recipe if you want to. Most kids will be happy with ketchup.

*****Two old timers were sitting on a bench griping about getting old. "You know this getting old really stinks," Murray says. "I always feel like I gotta pee and when I get there nothing comes out. And constipation! Let me tell you, sometimes I go two, three days without going." "You think that's bad?", Joe says. "Every morning at seven o'clock I take a dump." " I'd give a lung to be so regular," Murray says. "What the hell you complaining about?" "I don't get up till eight," Joe says.

BEEF AND MACARONIS IN RED SAUCE

OK, OK it's fucking beefaroni. I would just call it that but I was afraid of having my balls sued off. My ex-mother-in-law used to call it Doobly-Doots, though for what apparent reason I have no clue. Besides I can't envision myself announcing, "Hey everybody c'mon, sit down. The Doobly- Doots are ready."

You will need:

1 lb. chop meat

8 oz. of elbow macaroni

1 cup of sour cream

1 6oz. can of tomato paste

1/2 cup grated Parmesan cheese

1/4 cup sugar

1 tbsp. crushed garlic

1/2 tsp. oregano

1/2-tsp. parsley flakes

1/4 tsp pepper

3 cups of water

Cook the elbows until they are done. In the meantime, brown the beef with the garlic. While you're at it put the tomato paste, water, sugar, oregano, parsley, and pepper in a pot and let the flavors blend under a nice low flame for about 20 minutes. When the beef is cooked drain the fat and add the beef to the sauce. Stir it in and let it simmer for a couple of minutes. In a bowl mix the Parmesan Cheese and the sour cream together. Mix everything together. Now repeat after me, "C'mon everybody, the Doobly-Doots are ready."

*****A fireman comes home from work one day and tells his wife, "We have this system at work that seems to work fairly well. One bell we all get our gear, two bells, we head for the trucks, three bells and we're on our way. I think this could work well for our sex life. One bell, you get undressed, two bells, you get in bed. Three bells we fuck all night." The wife likes the idea and agrees to go along with it. That night as they head up to bed the husband says, "Bell one," and the wife gets undressed. "Bell two," he yells, and the wife gets into bed. "Bell three," he yells, and they commence to getting it on. After about three minutes the wife yells, "Bell four!" "What the hell is bell four?" the husband asks. The wife replies, "Roll out more hose, you're nowhere near the fire!"

Halloween is Kick Ass Dude! I don't even know who is under those masks.

LINGUINE in CLAM SAUCE

You know what they say, "Eat beef, live longer. Eat fish, love longer." I don't know if that's true or not, but it got me started on seafood about thirty years ago. If you are a borderline seafood eater, that is if you like it just once in a while, recipes like this are perfect for you. The taste of the seafood is there but there are so many other flavors that you are not overwhelmed by it.
You will need:
1 lb. of linguine
2 - 3 cans of chopped clams (depending on how much you like clams)
1/2 stick of butter
3 tbsp. crushed garlic
3 tbsp. olive oil
1/2 tsp. pepper
1/2 tsp. basil
1/2 tsp. oregano
1/4 cup grated Parmesan Cheese

Put the water on to boil for the linguine. When the water is boiling add the linguine. In a saucepan, under a low flame put the butter, garlic and olive oil. Warm them up for two or three minutes. Do not brown the garlic. Next open the clams and drain the liquid into a bowl. Stir into the saucepan the clams, pepper, basil and oregano. Add about 1/2 the clam juice to the pan. Drop the flame low and keep stirring until your linguine is ready. Drain the pasta and dump it into a bowl. Add your clam mix, sprinkle the Parmesan Cheese on it and mix. Arggh, that's it mates.

*****A guy gets into an elevator. Standing next to him is the largest man he'd ever seen. Suddenly the elevator jerks to a halt, the lights go out and a dim emergency light comes on. The little guy nervously nods to the big man. The big man says, "7' 6", 350 pounds, 20-inch dick, 3 pound left ball, 3-pound right ball. Turner Brown."

With that the little guy faints. When the big guy finally revives him he asks what happened. The little guy says "Well, what did you say?" The big guy repeats, "7'6", 350 lbs. 20-inch dick, and 3 lb. left ball, 3 lb. right ball. My name is Turner Brown. "Fuck," says the little guy, "I thought you said turn around."

The perfect mixture of alcohol, mo-peds and insanity. The cops loved this one.

FAJITAS

Fajitas are a nice change from everyday Mexican foods like tacos, or the newly popular quesadillas. When you order them in a Mexican restaurant the main ingredient, usually beef or chicken, comes out on a cast iron skillet that is just slightly hotter than molten lava. Along with that comes an assortment of small bowls that contain all the little accompaniments to toss in the tortilla with the main ingredient. In this recipe I did a mix of beef and chicken.

You will need:

1 lb. beef or chicken
12 small corn tortilla shells
8 oz. cheddar cheese
1 large onion
1 medium green bell pepper
1 medium red bell pepper
1 carrot
1 tbsp. chili powder
1 tbsp. cumin
2 tbsp. crushed garlic
1/3 cup cooking oil
1/4 tsp. pepper
1/2 cup water

Since most of us don't have a collection of skillets and bowls lying around the house I'll give you the directions the way I make them at home.

In a large frying pan brown the beef or chicken in the oil along with the spices. While the meat is browning Julienne slice the peppers and onions. Take a potato peeler and shave thin strips of carrot into the pepper and onion. When the meat is browned add the veggies and water. Simmer this until most of the liquid is gone. The veggies should be soft by now. Lay the shells out and distribute the desired amount on each shell with some cheese. Roll them up and serve. Or if you prefer, it's a great dish over rice.

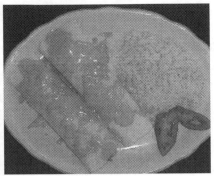

*****Three buddies decide they're going to start a business. Since their funds were not so strong they decide to go to Mexico where land and labor were cheap. They purchase a bungee-jumping rig and rent a piece of land on a cliff. After setting up the rig they decide to test it. A crowd of curious spectators gathered below. When all calculations were made Joe decides to give it a test run. Over the side he goes. On the first bounce up he is somewhat nicked up and shouting something to his friends, but he went by too fast. On the second bounce up he's very banged up and bleeding, but they still can't get him. On the third bounce they manage to pull his badly beaten body in. "What happened?" his friend asked. "Was the rope too short?" "No the rope's fine," Joe said. "But what the fuck is a Pinata?"

STUFFED EGGPLANT

This is a great dish that with little work will allow you to show off your culinary expertise. Even if you don't have any. If you can't get some after serving this, she's as frigid as the Fjords of the Arctic Circle. Hopefully you have some sauce on hand. If you don't I guess ya better make some.

You will need:

1 quart of tomato sauce
2 large eggplants
1 pint ricotta cheese
4 oz. mozzarella cheese
4 oz. chopped ham
1&1/2 cups breadcrumbs
2tbsps. grated parmesan cheese
1tsp. chopped basil
1/4 tsp. pepper
cooking oil

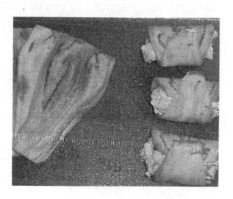

First slice the eggplant length wise into 1/4-inch slices. (Again, I recommend skinning them). Lightly brown them in a pan with some oil. While that's going on, dice the ham and mozzarella into 1/2-inch chunks. Mix together all the ingredients, except the breadcrumbs and tomato sauce. When the eggplant is done, fill each slice with the mix and roll them up. Put them in a baking tray, (lightly oil the tray), cover lightly with breadcrumbs and pour the sauce over them evenly. Cover the tray and cook in the oven at 350 degrees for 30 minutes.

**Bonus recipe! You can make the same dish with chicken instead of eggplant. You will just need about two pounds of chicken breasts. Pound the breasts real thin. Do not cook them. Stuff them raw. You may need a toothpick to hold them together. Follow the recipe for eggplant only you may have to cook them about 10 - 15 minutes longer.

*****A good buddy throws a surprise 25th wedding anniversary party for his best friend and his wife. Everybody is having a great time drinking, dancing and laughing. He looks over in a corner and there's his best friend sitting alone with his head buried in his hand. He walks over and the groom looks up with tears in his eyes. "What's the matter?" the best man asks, "A little overwhelmed?" "No, that's not it," the groom answers. "Remember the day I got married?" "Hell yeah," replies the best man. "Like it was yesterday. I remember how mad you got when you found the price tags for the gown, and the three hundred dollar bra, and the four hundred dollar shoes. Shit you were so mad you were gonna kill her." "Yeah, I know" the groom replied. "I'd be getting out tomorrow."

Hey, I got a good idea, let's have one more shot!
JOHN, RICH, BIG DAVE, ME, TY, TIM, KEVIN, RICK

SHRIMP AND SCALLOP KA-BOBS

All right mates, fire up the barbie. If it's winter, fire up the broiler. If you like seafood these little ka-bobs are better than sex, alone. Let's not get carried away. This recipe came to me one night in the form of a vision. A beautiful naked nymph stood before me holding a plate of shrimp and scallops. "Do you like what you see?" she asked. I told her yes, took the plate, went in the kitchen and started cooking. Damn drugs, they confuse your order of priorities. That's why I don't...nah, never mind you wouldn't believe me anyway.

You will need: (for a bunch)
1/2 lb. shrimp (good sized)
1/2 lb. bay scallops
1/2 lb. bacon
1 or 2 medium onions
1 or 2 medium tomatoes
1 clove of garlic
Old Bay seasoning
Barbeque sauce

Peel the shrimp. Slice halfway through each scallop and put a sliver of garlic in the center. Rub Old Bay seasoning on the shrimp and scallops. Lay the bacon out and cut the strips in half. Wrap one piece of bacon around each scallop. Slice the onion and tomatoes in pieces about the same size as the shrimp. Push the ingredients onto the skewer in any order or amount you like. Brush a bit of barbeque sauce over the ka-bob. Cook over an open barbeque or broil in the oven. When the bacon is done everything is done.

*****A religious man walks into the confessional and takes his knee. "Bless me Father, for I have sinned. I used the name of the Lord in vain" "Tell me about it my son," the priest says. "Well Father, the other day I was out golfing and shooting the game of my life. I came to the hardest hole on the course and hit an unbelievable drive. Then out of nowhere the wind picks up and carries my ball right into a tree." "Ah," says the priest. "No wait Father," the man interrupts. "The ball hit a branch and ricochets right into the middle of the fairway 50 yards further than it should have. So I calculate the wind and take my next shot for the green. Just as I hit the ball the wind stops and my ball goes right for the bunker." "Well that could make any man....." the priest says, and gets cut off in mid sentence. "No, not that Father," the man interrupts. "The sand was hard so my ball just ran through it, flipped up over the lip and landed six inches from the hole." "Christ," the priest replied. "Don't tell me you missed the fucking putt!"

BONES, A LADY FRIEND & ME

PASTA PRIMAVERA

This is another meatless dish that would be considered vegetarian except for the cheese and butter. I hate those purists. Anyway, it's a dish loaded with flavor that would probably be good for you Catholics on Friday during Lent. Actually it's good anytime.
You will need:
1lb. uncooked ziti
2 large tomatoes
1 small head of broccoli
1 stick of butter
1 bell pepper
1 zucchini
2 tbsps. chopped garlic
2 tbsps. grated Parmesan cheese
1 tsp. basil
1/2 tsp. salt
1/4 tsp. pepper
Olive oil

 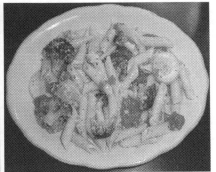

Timing is everything to make this dish work. You don't want your pasta to cool and you don't want your veggies to overcook so you have to time both sections of this recipe to be done simultaneously. In a pot bring four quarts of water to a boil. While that's happening you have plenty of time to: dice up the tomatoes and broccoli, slice the zucchini into 1/4 inch medallions and the pepper into thin strips. Once the water is boiling cook the pasta. At the same time, in a pan over a low flame, melt the butter and add the veggies and spices. Keep stirring while your cooking these. We don't really want to overcook the veggies. They should be fairly firm for this dish. If you're lucky, (and you probably will be) the pasta will be cooked about the same time the veggies are ready. When ready, drain the pasta and put into a good sized mixing bowl. Drizzle some Olive oil over the pasta and stir in for a nice light coat. Not too much as to have a puddle of oil on the bottom of the bowl. Add the cooked veggies, sprinkle the Parmesan over it all and stir. Hey if you want to get kooky I've added anything from chicken to pepperoni to fish into this dish and it still shines. Go on, get kooky!

*****I used to be's...
I used to be a baker, but I don't knead the dough anymore.
I used to be a fortuneteller, but I couldn't see a future in it.
I used to be an undertaker, but business was dead.
I used to be a doctor, but I didn't have the patients.
I used to be schizophrenic, no I wasn't.

DALE & PHILLY B.

CHICKEN CORDON BLEU

The French have a great way with language. Everything they say sounds sexy, sophisticated or dirty. Well, at least to me it does. Come on, think about it; Maurice Chevalier, Catherine Deneuve, Pepe le Pew. Same with this dish. Sounds complicated or exotic. Not. It's quite simple and easy to make. If my brudder Jo-Jo from Staten Island was to name it he'd call it "Ya know, that chicken wit da ham and cheese and shit. Wit da mushroom soup on it too." Which is exactly what it is.

You will need:
3 boned and skinned chicken breasts
1/2 pound of ham
1/2 pound of sliced Swiss cheese
1 ten oz. can of cream of mushroom soup
8 oz. mushrooms
1 cup of breadcrumbs
1/2 cup of flour
1 1/2 cup milk
1/2 stick of butter
1/3 cup of white wine

Split the chicken breasts down the middle and trim off all the nasty stuff like that vein looking thing in the middle. Now you have six half breasts. Place each breast between plastic and smash them down to about an eighth inch thickness. Lay the breasts out and put a slice of ham and a slice of cheese on each one. Roll them up and hold them closed with a toothpick. In a saucepan melt the butter. Put the flour in a small bowl, the eggs (beaten) in another, and the bread crumbs in a third. Now roll the chicken in the flour, dip it in the egg mixture, and roll it in the breadcrumbs. Lightly brown the coated chicken in the butter and place them in a baking tray. (*This would be a good time to remove the toothpicks unless you'd rather remove them from your dinner guests gums) Save the juice in the pan. Slice and cook the mushrooms in the same pan for a couple of minutes then add the soup and milk. Continue cooking until the soup and milk are well mixed. Turn off the flame and stir in the wine. Now pour this mix over the chicken and cook at 345 degrees for about 45 minutes. If you are serving this to a lady, not only will she be impressed with the dish but, if you'll practice this phrase, "Me montrer vos mesanges," she'll be putty in your hands. Translation - "Show me your tits," but don't tell her that.

*****A guy and his afternoon fling are heavily involved in sex when the phone rings. The woman goes over to the phone and after a brief conversation comes back and says, "That was my husband." "Well I guess I better get out of here," the guy says. "Relax," says the woman, "he's at the club playing cards with you."

BEEF BURGUNDY

This is a recipe that's great to whip out when apologies are in order. Come on, we all screw up sometimes. It's a great before make-up sex dish. Anyway, it's easy and the only thing that takes any time is waiting for the meat to get tender. The rest of the prep and cooking are fast.
You will need:
2lbs. beef chuck (get the stuff that's already been cubed. It saves time and is just about the same cost.)
2 large onions
8 oz. mushrooms
2 cups of red burgundy
1 tbsp. beef base
1 quart of water
1 cup of water
2 tbsps. flour
cooking oil
salt and pepper

Mix the beef base in the water and bring to a rapid boil. Cut the beef into one-inch chunks and put them in the boiling water. Here's where the time comes in. Let the beef boil until most of the water is evaporated. That's what makes it nice and tender. This might take about 45 - 60 minutes. (So go buy some flowers.) Now slice the onions and mushrooms into thin slivers and brown them in a bit of oil until they are soft. Use a good sized pan because you will be adding the meat and everything else to it. Once your water is cooked down, add it to the pan along with the burgundy. Whisk the two tbsps. of flour with a cup of warm water and slowly stir it into the pan. Turn the flame down and let it thicken and simmer for about 15 minutes. Serve it with her favorite side, like egg noodles or rice and some flowers. If this doesn't smooth things out you better sleep with one eye open and steel underwear on.

*****A guy is in one of those gigantic super marts shopping with his wife. For twenty minutes he's walking around in circles trying to find her. Finally, exasperated, he walks up to a woman and asks her if she would talk to him for a minute or two. The woman, a bit confused, asks why he would want her to talk to him. "Because," the man replied. "Every time I talk to a woman with tits like yours my wife shows up out of nowhere."

BEEF STEW

I suppose, just as with any recipe there are about a trillion ways to make beef stew. This is my favorite recipe and I don't get too many complaints when I serve it as a lunch special.
You will need:
6 - 8 quarts of water
2 lbs. beef stew meat
4 medium potatoes
4 carrots
1 medium onion
2 stalks of celery
1 tbsp. of beef base
1 tsp. crushed garlic
1/4 cup of flour
*Salt and pepper to taste

In a large pot bring six quarts of water to a boil. Add the beef base. When you buy the beef stew meat it usually comes in about two inch chunks. I recommend cutting them into about 1-inch chunks. They will cook faster and will be more tender. Put the beef in the boiling water and let it boil for about 1 1/2 hours. This gives you plenty of time to dice all the rest of the veggies and read a few of the important political articles in this month's Playboy or Penthouse. After the hour and a half add the veggies and continue cooking for another 30 minutes or until the veggies are soft. Whisk the flour into two cups of warm water. Add the mix to the stew and cook for about five more minutes. Salt and pepper to desired taste.

*****A guy with a big black eye takes his seat on a plane bound for Pittsburgh. He looks over at the guy sitting next to him and can't help but notice that he also has a black eye. Striking up a conversation he turns to the guy and says, "I notice you have a shiner too. Ya know, it's pretty funny how I got mine. Ya see, I was standing on line to get tickets for this flight and when I got up to the counter I see the chick at the ticket counter has a set of knockers on her like I ain't never seen. I mean the things are just bursting through the blouse. Being somewhat distracted I meant to say, 'Can I have two tickets to Pittsburgh,' but I accidentally said 'Can I have two pickets to Titsburg,' and she walloped me. So what happened to you?" "You're not gonna believe this," the guy replied. "Pretty much the same thing happened to me. This morning at breakfast I was sitting across from my wife of 20 years. I meant to say pass the cornflakes honey, but I accidentally said 'you ruined my life you fucking bitch.' "

33 the BOOMER BURGER

I love sports! All sports, but particularly baseball and football. I don't have a lot of heroes but I do have a few guys who I just plain dig everything about. Clapton is my God as far as music, and for sports it's hands down David Wells. It's just plain fun to watch him play the game. He and I love the same things in life, i.e. our kids, rock and roll, Harley Davidsons, beer and baseball. Other than the fact that Boomer's now a gazillionaire, we're like the same guy. Oh yeah, and maybe that perfect game thing. Man, that was a fucking work of art! So anyway Boomer, here's the perfect burger to honor your perfect game.

You will need: (for 4 -- 1/2 lb. burgers)

2lbs. ground beef (go for 90/10 c'mon, this is the perfect burger)

2 packs (1 box) dried onion mushroom soup mix

2 eggs

1/4 cup water

1/4 pound of your choice cheese (optional)

4 Good N.Y. style hard rolls (not stale rolls like they tried to give me down south)

Lettuce and tomato (optional)

Mix the ground beef, soup mix, eggs and water in a bowl. Patty up four good sized burgers. Toss them on the grill or on a really hot skillet or pan. *Big tip for making burgers; **DO NOT** keep squashing the burgers with the spatula. It doesn't make them cook any faster. All it does is dry them out. In fact the way I make them is to put them on the grill and cover them with a pan lid, and I've been told many times I've got the best burger around. Add the cheese if you please and re- cover. The cheese will melt very fast when covered. Toss 'em on a roll, add your extras and serve. The perfect burger to honor my man's perfect game. Stop by for one Boomer. I'm only an hour and change outside the stadium.

*****Two old guys, Dave and Roger, are sitting on a park bench listening to a ball game. Every day for fifteen years it was the same ritual, meet at the park, listen to the game, and talk baseball. One day Roger doesn't show up and Dave finds out that his buddy has passed away. Still Dave continues to go to the park and listen to the game. One day Dave hears a voice. "Dave," the voice says. "It's me, Roger. I'm up here in heaven and I've got some good news and some bad news for you." "What is it Rog", Dave asks. "Well," Roger says. "The good news is, it's just like we use to hope for. There is baseball in heaven and you get to play with whomever you like. Ruth, Gehrig, Mantle, they're all here." "What could be the bad news?" Dave asks "You're pitching tomorrow," Roger replies.

AARON, MARSHALL, dickhead, SLY and ME
13,500 and still alive
When given enough alcohol your balls will swell enough
to let you jump out of a plane.

TUNA NOODLE CASSEROLE

And yet another one of those great grade school cafeteria specials. This is a quickie that's healthy, fast and cheap. Three really big words in my house.
You will need:
2 6 1/2 oz. cans of tuna
1/2 medium onion
2 stalks of celery
1/2 cup mayo
1/4 tsp. salt
pinch of pepper
1/2 lb. elbow macaronis
6 oz. cheddar cheese
1 can of creme of celery soup
1 cup of milk
1 cup of bread crumbs

Preheat the oven to 400 degrees. Next boil up 4 quarts of water and cook the macaronis. While that's going on you need to open and drain the two cans of tuna and put them in a large mixing bowl. Dice the celery and onion and add them and the salt, pepper and mayo to the tuna. Mix it up good. Now put the milk, soup and cheese in a saucepan over a low flame. Heat this mixture until the cheese melts. Hopefully, by now or real soon, the elbows will be cooked. When they are, drain them and dump them in the bowl with the tuna. Add the melted cheese/soup mix to the bowl. Once again mix it all up nice and evenly. Put the whole shebang in a casserole-baking tray. Spread the breadcrumbs over the top, cover, and bake for 20 - 30 minutes at 400 degrees.

*****A guy is riding on a bus sitting next to a very beautiful young lady. Unfortunately she is dressed in the habit of a novice nun. The man looks over at her and says, "Boy, I'd sure like to make love to you and perhaps talk you out of becoming a nun." "Oh that's very sweet and flattering," the nun replied, "but I've devoted my life to God." She gets off the bus at the next stop. "Man," the guy says to the bus driver, "I'd sure love to fuck that!" "For $20 I'll tell you how you can," said the bus driver. The guy hands the bus driver $20. "OK," says the driver. "Every night she goes to the cemetery and prays for all the lost souls. You just have to get yourself a long dark robe and one of those glow in the dark masks go up to her and she'll think you're an angel or something." Later that night the guy shows up at the cemetery in his disguise. "Come to me and make love to me my child," he says. "Is that you Lord?" she says. "Yes, I'll make love to you but it must be anally for I must remain a virgin." So the guy has his way with her and when he's done he pulls off the mask and says, "Ha, jokes on you.

I'm the guy on the bus." "No actually," the nun says standing up and removing the habit. "The jokes on you. I'm the bus driver."

SHEPARD'S PIE

OK kids, here's an easy one that has it all in one dish. You got your meat, potato, veggies and dairy all rolled into one. And the kids will eat it too cause it's called pie!
You will need:
2 lbs. of ground beef
2 lbs. of potatoes
16 oz. of frozen or canned corn
6 oz. of shredded cheddar cheese
1 16oz. Can of tomato sauce
1/2 cup of milk
1 medium onion
1/2 stick of butter
1tsp. chopped garlic
Salt and pepper

All right now we're going to multi-task. Dice the

onion and put it in a pan with the beef and garlic. At the same time, put on about six quarts of water to boil. Peel and cut the potatoes into little chunks so they will cook faster. Put the potatoes in the boiling water and cook until tender. OK, back to the meat. When the meat is browned and the onions are tender drain the fat, and in a large bowl, combine the meat, corn and tomato sauce. Mix it up good. Salt and pepper to taste. Now back to the potatoes. When they are done mash them with the milk and butter. Hopefully you have an electric mixer. I recommend you buy one. All right, last step. Preheat the oven to 350 degrees. In a baking dish put the meat mixture on the bottom. Spread the mashed potatoes over the top and sprinkle the cheese over the potatoes. Cover and bake for 30 - 40 minutes.

*****A little girl is attending her first wedding. "Mommy," she asks. "Why is the bride dressed in all white?" "Because white is the color of happiness," the mom answered. "And today is the happiest day of her life." "So then," said the little girl. "Why is the groom dressed all in black?"

BREAKFAST

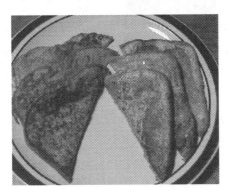

PANCAKES

Sing along everybody, *"Aunt Jemima's pancakes without her syrup, is like the spring without the fall...* That's right. I go with the old adage here; if it ain't broke, don't fix it. Aunt Jemima's Original, not, I repeat not, the complete, makes the best pancakes in the world. Hand's down, no questions, end of story. I do have a couple of minor adjustments. Only because me, and my kids like pan CAKES. The pancakes I make are over an inch high and fluffy.
You will need:
1 cup of Aunt Jemima's pancake mix
3/4 cup of milk
1 egg
2 tbsps. melted butter

In a bowl add the mix, milk and egg and whisk until blended. Pour the melted butter in and whisk some more. Heat the skillet or whatever cooking surface you use to 375 degrees. Aunt Jemima says *"Skillet is ready when drops of water sizzle, then disappear almost immediately."* Pour the batter on the skillet and turn over when bottom is golden brown. The secret to getting the cakes to rise real high is to turn them before the top gets too done. Once those little craters appear and the top gets dry it's too late for any rising action. By the way Aunt

Jemima says this amount of mix will make 10 - 12 pancakes. Aunt Jemima must have been from Biafra. I get 3 - 4 good-sized cakes out of this mix. *"There's only one thing worse, in the whole universe, and that's no Aunt Jemima at all."* Hey did you notice that Aunt Jemima lost the doo-rag? Bet she didn't know they'd be back in style.

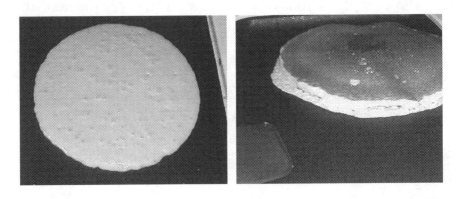

*****An Englishman, a Scotsman and an Irishman walked into a bar and each ordered a pint of beer. Just then some flies in the bar landed in each of their beers. The Englishman was disgusted and ordered a fresh beer. The Scotsman picked the fly out of his beer and continued drinking. The Irishman reached into his beer, grabbed the fly by the wings and shouted, "Spit it out you bastard!"

MUSHROOM OMELET

OK, here's a beauty that I just had to add to this book. The beauty lies in the fact that I really don't have to include a joke after the recipe. It comes from my best buddy who has an even more bizarre sense of humor (lying beneath the cool exterior) than I do. Basically, it cracked me the fuck up. It came in the form of an e-mail and here it is, verbatim.

Dear Roger,

I understand you are writing another cook book and would like to have my easy to make mushroom omelet in this addition...(I believe he meant edition but like I said this is verbatim) it's easy and tastes great!... Just takes two eggs, mushrooms, a teaspoon of milk and some butter. Beat two eggs, some chopped mushrooms and a dash of milk in a small bowl. Butter your pan with the heat on medium and pour egg mixed with mushrooms in pan, cook till you can flip, and enjoy!

thank you for considering this tasty food for your book.

Phillyb

*Hey Philly, that Emeril guy can't shine your shoes!

FRENCH TOAST

I didn't do too many breakfast recipes in this book because, um, actually I don't know why. Oh well, I hope you enjoy the few I did write.

You will need: (4 - three slice servings)

12 slices of bread

4 eggs

1 cup of milk

1 tbsp. of cinnamon

2 tbsp. butter for mix

1 tsp. of vanilla extract

1 tbsp. butter for pan

 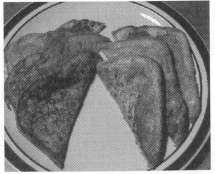

In a bowl mix the eggs, milk, vanilla and half the cinnamon. Melt the butter and add to the mix. Before you start dipping the bread make sure the mix was just stirred. The cinnamon has a way of floating to the top and you could o.d. on cinnamon if you get it all on one slice. In fact give a quick stir before each dipping. Dip each slice on both sides for about 3 seconds. When you get half the bread done put the rest of the cinnamon in the mix and stir. Butter the pan and cook over a medium flame until they are golden brown.

*****Time flies like the wind. Fruit flies like bananas.

McCABE'S FLAG FOOTBALL TEAM
UNDEFEATED REGULAR SEASON 1993

HUEVOS RANCHEROS

Literally translated it means ranch eggs. We know that the Mexican's like their food with a little kick. So do I. Just not usually for breakfast. But in the case of this recipe it's perfect for those morning after days. This recipe should not even be considered unless you have some leftover salsa lying around. So remember when you're partying stash a cup or two in the fridge behind the salad dressings. All right boys, let's sweat those toxins out!

You will need: (for each serving)

2 eggs

1/2 cup of salsa

1 slice of butter

1 or 2 slices of ham

1/4 cup of grated cheddar cheese

Butter the bottom of a saucepan and put on a low flame. Pour the salsa in the pan. When it begins to simmer, spread a space in the middle and add the eggs. Ladle some of the salsa over the top off the eggs. Place the ham and cheese over the eggs and cover for about one minute or until the eggs are the way you like them. Remember, once the eggs go in the whole thing moves pretty quickly. You don't -- well, I don't, want my yokes dried out.

*****A guy gets into an elevator and in the process of reaching to press the floor button he accidentally brushes up against a woman's breast with his elbow. "I'm sorry, he says, but I know if your heart is as soft as your breast you'll forgive me." "Honey," the woman replied, "if your dick is as hard as your elbow I'm in room 363."

Yeah, we can tear up a course
JOE, MIKE, NOKE, ME

FOR THE KIDS

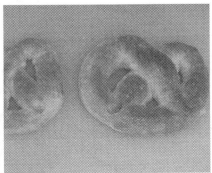

FRENCH BREAD PIZZA

This is a real like, "Shit! I gotta feed these kids and get down to the bar for kick-off in less than 1/2 hour," recipe. So I'll make it quick.
You will need: (makes 4 pizzas)
2 loaves of French bread
1 eight once jar or can of tomato sauce
8 oz. of shredded mozzarella
1 tbsp. chopped garlic
dried parsley

Preheat the oven to 450 degrees. Cut the bread in half and split them lengthwise. Layer the bread in this order. Garlic, tomato sauce, cheese, and sprinkle a bit of parsley over the top. Stick it in the oven for 10 - 12 minutes, or until the cheese is melted. If you're in a real hurry, and you have a decent sized toaster-oven, you can do 2 slices at a time in about three minutes. I do.

*****A group of kids were in their second week of first grade. "OK," the teacher said, "I want each of you to tell me what they did over the weekend, but I want you to speak like grown-ups. You're not little babies anymore. Suzie, what did you do over the weekend?" "I went to visit my nana," Suzie replied. "That's nice Suzie," the teacher said, "but we want to use big words. You went to visit your grand-ma. Ok Billy, what did you do this weekend?" "I went for a ride on a choo-choo," Billy replied. "No Billy," the teacher said. "You went for a ride on a train. Let's get used to using big words." "Johnny," the teacher asked, "what did you do this weekend?" "I read a book," Johnny answered. "Very good," the teacher said. "And what book did you read?" Johnny bowed his head, thought for a moment, looked up and said, "I believe that would be Winnie the shit."

PRETZELS

Remember when you used to go into the city and get those big ole soft pretzels from the vendors on the side of the road or at a ball game. They were so fresh and nice and warm coming right off the heater on the cart. Well forget it. Those days are gone forever. Any pretzel vendor with any pride has retired or died. I spent two days in New York City walking around looking for a decent pretzel. The soggy or stale pieces of shit they sell now aren't worth a dime, never mind the $3 - $4 they want at a game. 3 or 4 Bucks!!! I can make 60 fresh, jumbo, delicious old time pretzels for the price of one 5lb. sack of flour and 4 eggs, which is roughly $2.00.
Besides all that stuff that pisses me off, this is a great project to do with your kids. There's nothing to it, it's a lot of fun, and no matter how big a mess you make it all wipes up with a damp sponge. So go get the kids and lets have some fun!
You will need:
4 cups of flour
1 package of active dry yeast
1 egg
2 tbsp. of sugar
1 tsp. of salt
1 1/2 cups of warm water

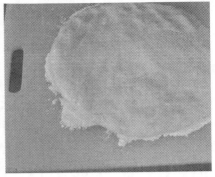

In a bowl mix the yeast, sugar and salt with the warm water. Gradually stir in the flour to make a dough. Keep the bag of flour handy. When the mix starts getting doughy coat your hands with flour and remove it from the bowl. Put a little flour on your working surface. This keeps the dough from sticking to everything. Knead the dough for about ten minutes, shape it into a ball, and put it in a greased bowl. (I keep that spray shortening around to make life easier.) Roll the dough around the bowl so the whole exterior is lightly coated. Cover the bowl and place it in a warm area for about 50 minutes. The dough should double in size. Take it out of the bowl after it has risen, punch it down and let it sit for another ten minutes. Now cut off chunks of dough, roll them out and stretch them in strips about 1/2" around by 18" long. Make your cute little pretzel shapes and place them on a greased pan. Whisk the egg and brush each pretzel with the egg mix. Salt the pretzels and bake them in the oven at 350 degrees for 15 minutes, or until they are golden brown.

 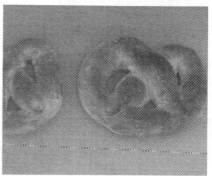

PIZZA DOUGH

The recipe I use is exactly the same as pretzel dough only I use half (1 tbsp.) the sugar. Follow the directions all the way. After you have punched the dough down and let it sit the ten minutes, cut it in two and stretch for two pies. Any unused dough can be frozen for future use. Now you can make pretzels and pizza. You sir, are an amazing dad.

*****A guy intent on getting his Sunday morning round of golf in with his buddies tiptoes out of the bedroom, quietly dresses, and heads off for the course. Upon arriving there, the skies open and all play is suspended. Since it was still the wee hours of the morning when he gets home, he figures he'll just sneak back into the house get undressed, slip in along side his wife, and perhaps get a little. He snuggles up against his wife's butt and whispers, "Boy, it sure is a lousy day out there." "Sure is," the wife replies. "Can you believe my asshole husband's out there playing golf in this?"

WE LOVE THE BEACH

STRAWBERRY SHORTCAKES

I'm not big on desserts mostly cause I'm such a pig at dinner there's no room left for dessert, and most desserts don't go well with beer. I do occasionally indulge in the sweets. This is a sweet treat you can whip up in about ten minutes.

You will need:

1 eight pack of dessert shells(available at any grocery store)

1 pint of fresh strawberries

1 tbsp. sugar

1 tbsp. light corn syrup

1/4 cup water

2 tbsps. Chambord Liqueur (optional, but worth it)

* For the whip cream

8oz. heavy cream

1 tbsp. sugar

1 tsp. vanilla flavoring

 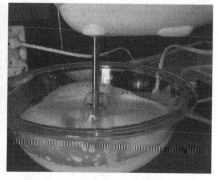

Cut the strawberries into small pieces. Put the strawberries, water, corn syrup and sugar in a saucepan. Simmer over a medium flame. When the liquid begins to thicken lower the flame, add the 2 tbsps. of Chambord and simmer for about two minutes. Remove the pan from the flame and pour into a bowl. Place the bowl in the fridge to cool.

To make whip cream pour the heavy cream, sugar and vanilla flavoring in a bowl. With an electric mixer whip on high speed for about 3 - 4 minutes or until you have a nice thick cream.

Lay your dessert shells out and spoon some whip cream in each. Take the strawberry mix out of the fridge and spoon some over the cream. Drizzle any leftover juice over the top. Me, on the other hand; I'm trying to watch my boyish figure so I eliminate the dessert shells and eat it straight out of my lady's navel.

***** Two guys are out on the golf course getting very angry at the slow pace the twosome ahead of them were playing at. As they're leaning against the cart waiting to make the next shot one finally says, "Stay here with the balls. I'm gonna go up and give those two broads a piece of my mind." He takes off and heads to the two ladies. About three-quarters of the way there he makes an abrupt u-turn and heads back. "What the hell happened?" The other guy asks. "I got just about to them and I saw that it was my wife and she was playing with my mistress." "Well shit," the other guy says. "I'll go up and tell them to let us through." Off he heads to the ladies and about three-quarters of the way there he does an abrupt u-turn. "Why'd you stop?" His partner asked. "Small world" he replied.

SUGAR COOKIES

If you told me we needed to work on my bike in order to obtain better emissions I might not be too interested. Now if you told me we needed to work on the bike to increase the horsepower I'd be up to my ass in oil and wrenches. Same goes for the kids. Tell them you're going to teach them how to properly Julienne cut onions you'll have to pry them off the couch. Tell them you're making cookies and they'll be up to their necks in flour and eggs. It's a fun project to do with the kids. I know I've been there. Give it a whirl, the kids will love it.
You will need:
1 cup of sugar
1 stick of butter
2 eggs
3 cups of flour
1 tsp. baking soda

First blend the butter and sugar together. Next, add in the eggs and salt. Keep mixing until it starts getting kinda fluffy. Lastly, stir in the flour and baking soda and mix until you have a uniform stiff mix. Put the dough in the fridge for an hour or two. When it's chilled roll it into a log shape and slice it into 1/4" slices. Place on a greased cookie sheet and bake for 8 - 10 minutes at 375.

DANIELLE AND NICOLE
When we made cookies

AFTERWORD

Laughter is one of the best things in life. Nothing makes me feel better than a good belly shaking, tear running, breath grasping laugh. It's better than sex, well some sex. I chose to surround myself with funny people. Most of my buddies are a fucking riot. When we all get together it's a guaranteed blast. So it only seems fitting that the last little bits of humor should be words of wit that came out of their mouths.

*****Many years ago when we were hippies and all driving around in our custom "love machines", that is vans, my buddy Mike came home in the wee hours of the morning and stumbled into bed. His girlfriend was getting ready for work and decided to have a quick look in the van for any incriminating evidence. Sure enough she found some. (Hey, I never said we were saints). She storms back into the house and starts clobbering Mike with a woman's shoe she found. "Who's shoes are these?" she demands to know. "I don't know", Mike replies through a fog. "What size are they?"

*****Another guy I know, Mitch Juron, was traveling back from a business trip with his boss. He was cruising down the highway clocking about eighty five miles an hour in a fifty five zone. Sure enough a trooper picks him up on the radar and pulls him over. "I've been waiting for you all day", the trooper says. "Well officer", Mitch replies, "I got here as fast as I could". Ticket dismissed. Even the cop had to love that one.

JO JO AND ME
The night guys since 1991

ABOUT THE AUTHOR

Hi. I'm Roger Cortes, the author of this book. At the request of the publishers I'm going to tell you a little "About the Author".

I was born in Da Bronx, N.Y. into a family of seven children. We ran out of room in the city and moved up to suburbia where I spent my "formative years".

At 13 I got my first job working at a summer resort called Davie's Lake. I quickly figured out that working in the kitchen was a far better place to be than picking up trash or baking in the sun in a large open field showing people where to park. From the age of 13 to 18 I worked my way up the ranks from scraping baking pans to preparing dinner for up to 1000 guests.

After two years in the army I spent the next fifteen years floating around the country playing rock and roll, working construction, tending bar and cooking. I finally settled down, (somewhat), got married, had two beautiful girls and bought myself a bar/restaurant.

I've been a writer all my life having been published in song, poetry and short story writing. This is my first complete book. Someday I'll finish the other four.

I currently reside in Ferndale, N.Y., a small town in the heart of the once famous "Borscht Belt" Catskill Mountains, where I still own and operate my places, McCabe's and Warehouse III.